# Tales
# from the
# "Voyage of Vagus V"

# Tales
## from the
## "Voyage of Vagus V"

## Reflections on a Sailing Adventure

## Lake Ontario to the Bahamas

by

**James Lait**

2008
OneOff Enterprises

**Canadian Cataloguing in Publication Data**

Lait, James, 1948-
  Tales from the "Voyage of Vagus V"

ISBN 978-0-9809011-0-8

1. Lait, James, 1948- -- Journeys. 2. Vagus V (Yacht). 3. Voyages to the Bahamas. 4. Yachts and Yachting. 5. Travel. 1. Title

G440.C664A3 2007          910.4' I


OneOff Enterprises
Burlington, ON, Canada
e-mail: oneoffenterprises@gmail.com

This is my story, so these pages are the result of my memory of events from my viewpoint. While my memory is good, it is not perfect so there may be other versions of events out there. Real names and boat names have been used where permission has been granted from the individuals for use. Names and boat names have been changed in cases where I have been unable to contact the individuals involved.

*To*

*Karen, my partner*

*in cruising and in life*

# Contents

# Acknowledgements

Thank you, thank you, thank you very much.

# Prologue

*Let's buy us a boat,*
*A life of romance.*
*Together we'll float*
*On a boat that will dance*
*On the waves so gentle,*
*In a breeze so warm,*
*Under the stars*
*In the embrace of your arms.*

*Float to the left, float to the right,*
*Sails up, sails down, it feels so right.*
*Here's to Romance!  Here's to Romance!*

*- Karen Lait -*

*A*ny man who has been married for a number of years and has a sailboat knows that he has not one, but two, Princesses in his life. Both Princesses require large amounts of attention, energy and time. Either one can instill in him a sense of peace and understanding and rightness with the world ... or make him utterly miserable. So when a sailboat enters the picture, life becomes a bit of a balancing act. He soon realizes that his happiness level is dependent on maintaining the teeter-totter of life on an even keel, so to speak. Occasionally the stars align and the two Princesses combine forces. This is about to happen as I find myself sailing off into the sunset with my wife Karen aboard our sailboat *Vagus V*. Karen's song would take on life.

# Leaving

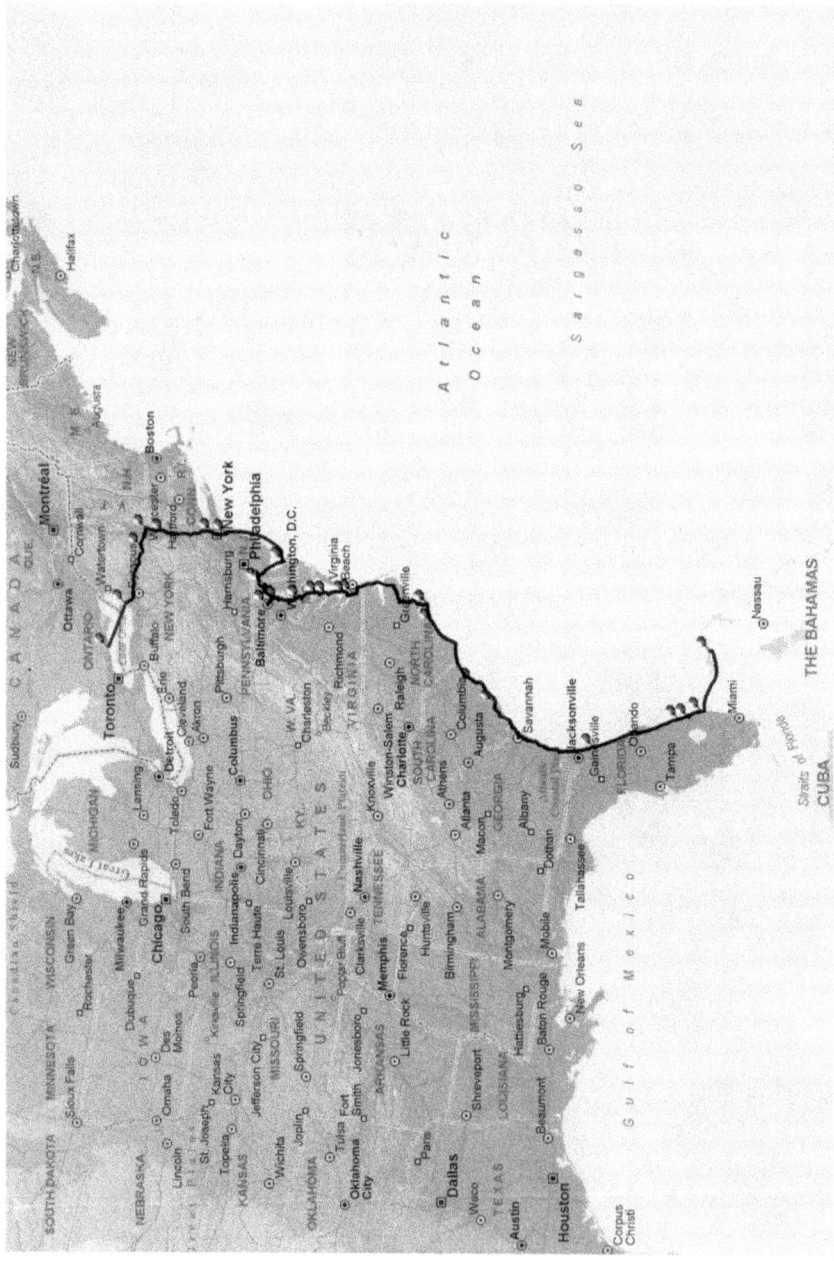

Our route from Lake Ontario to the Bahamas

# 1. In The Beginning

*T*he evening sun shone brightly as we slipped our dock lines for an overnight sail across Lake Ontario - destination: Oswego, New York. Oswego would be our first stop on a trip through the canals of New York, down the Hudson River, through Chesapeake Bay, along the Intracoastal Waterway (ICW) and on to the Bahamas and the Caribbean. Once underway and ready to sail, Karen went below to try to get a little rest. Gazing down through the companionway, I watched as she tried to settle on the settee. The boat gave a little lurch from an errant wave and, as I grabbed the binnacle for support, I thought, "This is going to be like living in a thirty-six foot hallway. But, a hallway with a difference." It's true. A sailboat moves - not always in a gentle to-and-fro manner, but more often in a jerky, unpredictable motion. A motion usually only experienced on rides in amusement parks. In fact, once one has been sailing, amusement parks lose their appeal. A sailor really has "been there" and "done that". Combine the close quarters and unpredictable boat motion with the reality of no hot showers, limited water supply, and the management of holding tanks, and life takes on new dimensions.

I glanced down at Karen again.

"How did we come to be doing this?" I mused. It all started when Karen turned forty. Prior to her birthday, which I had written on every calendar in the house and at work, Karen announced that she would like to go sailing. She used to watch sailboats from the beach, gently gliding through the water, occupants reclining leisurely in the cockpit. It looked like fun and a very nice way to travel. She had found an ad for an Open

House at a local sailing school with an offer to take people on a free introductory sail. As the date was on her birthday and the price was right, I readily agreed. It sounded like fun and a different way to celebrate her fortieth. Off we went on the Saturday morning of her birthday to the Open House and got in the queue for the sailboat ride. Soon we were seated on a C&C 27 with an instructor and several other guests.

Once the boat cleared the harbour and the sails were set, the instructor asked, "Who wants to steer?"

Everyone went quiet; everyone except, of course, me, who happily blurted, "It's her birthday today!" while pointing excitedly at Karen.

I promptly received one of those looks that a husband gets used to as the instructor insisted Karen take the wheel. Just as she grasped the wheel, the wind filled in. The sailboat heeled over and took off like a racehorse. Everyone scrambled to hang on, grabbing any nearby protrusion. The sudden surge of power from nothing but the gentle wind on the sails was exhilarating. And there was Karen, holding onto the wheel with both hands, the boat slicing through the water, with one of the widest grins on her face that I had ever seen. That moment was the start of our adventure.

It would be many years before we would actually leave. We had to learn to sail, make sure the kids grew up, purchase and prepare a sailboat, and work enough years to retire. These, however, were fun years for one can travel anywhere by imagination. I slowly started accumulating sailing magazine subscriptions. Each magazine offered a slightly different view on the adventure that awaited us; at least, that was the rationalization. The magazines showed all the latest boats and gadgets, as well as the latest places to take a boat. Plans on destinations were discussed, debated, changed and filed. Boat types were reviewed. Every book that mentioned sailing was borrowed from the public library to while away the winter nights. Those that sailed the oceans full time offered advice on how to do it cheaply, or without any electrical systems (keep it simple), or with every electronic gadget available. How to sail in storms, how to avoid storms, how to anchor, how to provision - name a "how to" and there were several articles to be had. Seminars by people who "had done it" were attended and notes reverently taken. The annual boat show was eagerly awaited to see and feel the new boats and to gawk at the wealth of sailing accessories available. The choices were endless but, for a long time, no serious decisions were necessary. It was a time of absorbing, of seeing how others had sailed off into the sunset, of trying to see what would be right for us and of asking ourselves whether we really wanted to undertake this adventure. These were all important steps along the road to new horizons. Now we were on the way!

*The day we left our homeport*

*LaSalle Park, Burlington, ON*

# *2. Preparation*

*I* checked my watch – time to record our position in the log book. Going below, I could hear Karen softly sleeping on the settee. We were well out into the lake and night had descended. We were motoring through light waves; the autopilot guiding *Vagus* on a heading for Oswego. After completing the log entries, I grabbed a granola bar and climbed out to the cockpit. No lights appeared on the horizon - nothing on the radar. Settling into a corner of the cockpit, out of the way of the breeze, I opened the wrapper. As I bit into the bar, I thought back over our years of preparation. How did we get here?

## *What to Bring?*

*L*ists, lists and more lists - if there is one thing that I like, enjoy, look forward to, and even savour, it is making a good list. When I discovered that one of the main ingredients in planning an escape into the sunset involved making a good list, I joyously waltzed off to the nearest office supply store in search of the perfect notebook.

"A proper list", I reasoned, "cannot be made on any old scrap of paper." At the store I found an array of notebooks in different sizes, shapes, colours and, of course, costs. The choice would be difficult. I really ought to have made a list of all the important attributes for a decent List Notebook before leaving home. I knew it should not be too big, as I would have to carry it around. One never knew when a fresh thought would surface that required jotting down. The pages should be lined as that would keep things neat and avoid upward or downward slants to the writing. Still pondering the options, I felt that the pages should be removable without affecting the rest of the book.

There were now three criteria for the book. Three, from past experience, rapidly approached the maximum number of ideas that I could safely hold in my head at once without a written list. Quickly scanning the shelves, cost jumped to the forefront of my bemused mind. Many of the notebooks were obviously designed for someone with an expense account. This notebook, I hoped, would be purchased with *some* of the grocery money, not all of it. I needed an inexpensive, practical notebook. Looking around, over in a corner, away from the leather-bound, daily itinerary books holding elegant pages for teeny-weeny writing ("Ah! Large line spacing should also be added"), I found a 14x9cm, relatively inexpensive, spiral-bound notebook. It had 200 sheets of paper, lined both sides. One edge had perforations to allow easy paper removal. It had a flexible cover so it could be shoved in a jacket pocket, and it came in a manly navy blue colour (another criterion). Eureka! Now I could record all those important thoughts, ideas and suggestions that I came across while preparing for the trip.

While on my way to the checkout, I realized I would also need a proper pen to record all those pearls of wisdom and priorities of life. Off I trotted to the pen aisle. With horror I gazed at more pens and pen types than I ever imagined could exist. By this time, store clerks would peer down the aisle at me, smile, shake their heads and walk away quickly. However, this time, I got lucky. Directly ahead, just where I happened to stop, was a package of three pens. They were proper click-type pens so I would not lose the end cap. A sleek silver with ergonomically designed, soft rubber finger grips, they had a metal ballpoint tip, 0.7mm in diameter, and used liquid gel ink. I was not sure what liquid gel ink meant or the relative benefits of the composition of the ball, but the pens looked good. They looked like proper pens for making serious lists.

Lists that could be followed and would lead us on the adventure of a lifetime. A pen I could take out with my list book, click open and state, "Let me jot that down" and people would think, "There goes an organized man." Happiness! I purchased the pens and notebook – actually, at that price, two notebooks. I would surely go through one quickly with all the lists that needed making. Elatedly, with the feeling that I had just taken a major step along the road called Life, I hopped in the car and headed for home, completely forgetting that I was supposed to pick up groceries on the way. It would be an order-in pizza night.

After our pizza dinner, I was set. I had my list notebook and I had my list pens. Sitting in my favourite chair in the family room, I got a pen out of the package, tested it to make sure it wrote freely, and opened the list notebook. On the front page I carefully scribed the name of our boat, "*Vagus V*" - so far so good. I then wrote the year, for it would be several years before we could leave and I would likely use at least one book a year. Then came our phone number in the hope that if the book was ever misplaced or lost, some kind soul would realize its true value and call. And with all these important lists, the book would be priceless. I leaned back and looked at the first page. It looked good. Only 199 pages left. What next? Suddenly inspired, I realized that I should write out the lists I wanted to make - a List of Lists. So on the second page, in large letters across the top, I wrote LISTS. Now what next? Karen brought in tea.

"What are you doing?" she asked.

Proudly I replied, "I am making a list in preparation for our trip."

"Oh, good idea," she said, thinking that it would at least keep me busy.

It was amazing. It was an epiphany. When anyone asked what I was doing, I would tell them I am making a list. It was a socially acceptable thing to do. People would go away happy in the knowledge I am going about something useful and would not ask me to clean the rug or take out the garbage.

"Don't disturb your father. He is making a list." - I could hear those words already. There were rewards to list making.

Once again I stared at a blank page. "Well, I need a To-Do list. One always needs a To-Do list. Of course it will need to be prioritized: items that we Absolutely-Have-To-Do-Or-We-Are-Not-Leaving, Must-Do, Like-To-Do, and Wish-To-Do." This was a good start. "And I will need a To-Buy list. This list can be subdivided by store so whenever I get to that particular store I can whip out my handy List Notebook and be ready to embark on the required purchases. Oh – and I will need a To-Take list. This list should cover spare parts for the engine and for the boat, books, clothing, medical supplies, emergency equipment, and provisions. I should also have a category called Places-To-Go. After all, that is the point isn't it? We are going to go some place. All the rest is just the means." This indeed was a good start. I was happy. It was a step. It might be a tiny step but it was a step. I could now spend countless winter evenings pouring through magazines and books, cruising the Internet, making and revising lists.

Karen also got into the spirit of the lists. I looked to be having so much fun that she thought that she should also have a try. She chose the topics of provisioning, medical supplies and the abandon ship bag contents as hers. She chose the provisioning list because she quite rightly felt it would fall to her anyway, and she thought that pizza would not always be readily available where we were going. Medical supplies, because she has a medical background and at least recognizes some of the words. She realized that my idea of a medical supply kit was a liberal supply of bandages. The abandon ship bag sort of became hers. She was not sure why but it seemed to be a good idea at the time. She would of course regret all three choices.

The provision list should have been easy, but Karen made the fundamental mistake of researching the topic instead of going with her basic instincts. Her basic instincts would have saved a lot of effort and anxiety and were probably just as correct. Most of the articles and books she read were about people sailing off into the sunset, going to far away places where flour, let alone pizza, was difficult to obtain. So provision lists involved stocking the boat for six month self-sufficiency without ever having to grace the doors of a supermarket. The books were united in the proposition; one must have supplies. In fact, Karen's reasoning ran along the lines that, basically, people must eat. So if one is traveling to places where there are people, one must be able to get things to eat. Albeit she might not be able to get her favourite brand of peanut butter, but she was going to new places and could experience new foods. She should still be able to eat. Karen was right. But how could she be right against all this collective wisdom? She prepared lists of provisions that would have sunk the boat, revised these lists, questioned ever leaving, and finally reached a compromise. She decided to look at the trip as a series of two-week vacations. She made a list that covered their needs for two weeks then added in extras of staples that one does not like to carry home from a supermarket. To this she added two weeks supply of long life meals – food in cans and hiker meals. This was the emergency food. Food that we could eat if we were desperate (and she really hoped that we would never be that desperate). We ended up giving most of this food away after the first year of cruising.

The medical supplies followed in a similar vein. Once again she was confronted with reams of lists, procedures, and medicines that were absolutely essential for six-crew boats sailing non-stop around the world. One should not leave home without these supplies. Once again her basic instincts were right. People get injured and sick. There were doctors out there where there were people. So basically she decided to bring what we could comfortably use, with a few exceptions. She made her list and went over it with her doctor who gave her blessing. The local pharmacist, after getting over the initial shock, happily showed her how to use an epi-pen. Her proudest addition to the medical kit though, her piece-de-resistance, was a catheter for me. This item is apparently a very important piece of equipment if we are on a long offshore passage and things get blocked, so to speak.

"A man can only live three days without peeing," she stated, as I immediately scrunched my legs together. "What size should I get?"

"They come in different sizes?" I responded shakily.

"Oh yes," said Karen, "they come in three different diameters." Hoping to make me feel more manly, she added, "I thought I should get you the largest one."

"In this instance," I gulped " I think that the small one will suffice." This medical item became a lively topic of conversation among the women at the annual boat club Christmas Party.

The abandon ship bag was not fun. Karen found it depressing. Here, about to embark on the trip of a lifetime on her sailboat, she had to think about what we would need if we had to get off the boat in a hurry. Not a pleasant thought for a winter's eve. Karen quickly realized that the problem with most Abandon Ship lists that people produce is that, if she bought everything on the list, the items would not only fill our boat but would definitely be too heavy to carry when scrambling over the side of a sinking ship. The list had to be pared down, but what to take? It was tough. She could just imagine bobbling along in the life raft when she thought, "I need a left-handed can opener", only to realize that she had pared that item from the list. Our very survival could depend on that item! There was no easy answer. All she could do was take her best shot at it, pray she would never need it, and get on to something else before she got totally depressed. Something like, "What clothing should I take?" Ah, there was nothing like another list to bring her out of the doldrums and give her new challenges. Karen had an out. This she would enjoy.

## *Das Boat*

*W*e were lucky and found a good, ocean-capable sailboat that we could just barely afford. We had put a lot of effort into scanning the sailing magazines, visiting the boat shows, agonizing over the various boat designs, keel shapes, sail design, stability factors, and stowage capabilities before realizing we had not a glimmer of hope of affording anything that we saw. Perhaps by selling the house and sending our children off into indentured servitude we might have a chance of buying something new in a small basic model.

Eventually our diligence paid off and we felt great delight when a local broker spotted a boat for us. The 20 year old boat, although needing a lot of cosmetic work, came from a good pedigree. The survey came out well and after a bit of negotiation, we owned *Vagus V*. The purchase went through in October. By this time the boat had been lifted out for the winter season and was buried in a boatyard in the Thousand Islands. We, on the other hand, lived at the opposite end of Lake Ontario - about a four-hour drive away.

"No problem," said I, forever the optimist. Karen would grow to shudder at these words in the coming years. The words would take on a very different meaning for her than for me.

"No problem," said I, "we can drive down in the spring, commission the boat and sail her back. We can take a series of fun weekends getting the boat ready. I will make a list of all that has to be done. Not to worry."

Now we have been married for a number of years and Karen thought she knew me. However, she was not prepared for what happened when a sailboat was thrown into the equation. Things changed. For example, she did not immediately see that the once cautious, conservative husband she had grown to know, the one to whom she used to say, "Don't be so negative!" had morphed into a raving optimist. She soon learned. That winter, as we settled into our cold weather lives, we looked forward to the spring when we would proudly sail our new boat into our home marina. We were blissfully unaware of the trials that lay before us before we could bring the boat home. This was a major step. We now had the boat for our trip. We just had to pay for it, fix it up and it would be ready to go. "No problem," I re-iterated as I settled into a nice round of list making.

Six years later, we were on our way South. Looking back on those years, I realized that one needed three ingredients to prepare a boat for going south, once again keeping to my rule of three's. The first and most important is time, the second is a good book and third, a nice supply of bandages.

*Vagus* required a little tender loving care before sailing off into the great unknown. Not major jobs but a lot of the systems such as hosing, rigging, wiring and cushions were tired and needed replacing. There were also all those "must have" goodies like GPS, radar and ham radio system, carefully researched during the winter months, that needed to be installed.

Karen soon learned to translate my boat job time estimates. A two hour job meant at least half a day, a half day job meant two days, and a one day job meant that she did not expect to see me for a week and she better lay in some groceries. The sad fact is boat jobs take time, a lot of time. I found that nothing is standard and nothing is easy to get at without taking something else apart. I always seemed to be in the middle of the job when I would discover that I was missing a crucial part, a part that required a trip to the local chandler. The local chandler would typically be out of this particular part (obviously a popular part), and, as it would invariably now be late on a Saturday afternoon, I would arrive at the next chandler just after closing time. On top of that, the part usually came in at least two sizes and I would not be sure which size actually fit. Initially, I got very frustrated with the lack of progress. And Karen got very frustrated with me whenever I said, "It'll just be a quick job."

Karen also came to realize that any job on a boat meant tearing the boat apart. Parts, tools, cushions and items previously neatly stored in lockers soon became spread around the cabin as I tried to install a particular gadget. I have a good friend, Daryl, who is able to work on a job without creating a disaster zone. When Daryl works, all his tools stay neatly in the tool case and parts are neatly arranged in order of assembly. This never worked for me. I tried. I would carefully set out the tools, arrange parts, rearrange the contents in the lockers under attack and, within twenty minutes, it would look as if the boat had been turned upside down and shaken. I have no idea how this would happen. I took to watching Daryl working on his boat, carefully taking notes on procedure in my notebook. It did not help. I then invited Daryl over to watch me work and give me pointers. But as I started working, Daryl's mouth quickly disconnected from his brain, his eyes got wider and, after five minutes, he muttered "I can't take any more," and disappeared. After that incident, Daryl would only help me if Daryl did the work. Not a bad arrangement.

Karen realized there was a problem. She was usually around when I was working. She tried to do some of the jobs that I had so neatly put on her list. She would start a job only to find her workspace getting smaller and smaller. Soon she could barely move as the boat filled with tools, displaced locker stuff and cushions that had to be moved. In frustration she would go over to Daryl's boat to have a beer with her friend, Ann, who was often to be found reading quietly in the cockpit of her boat. Soon Karen skipped the idea of working on her own boat whenever I announced work to be done. She just trotted over to Daryl and Ann's boat.

"Jim working again?" said Daryl.

"Yes" said Karen.

"Do you think he needs help?" said Daryl.

"He always needs help," sighed Karen, "but there won't be any room to help." The times on her friend's boat gave Karen an idea.

"Jim," she said, "I think we should have a little talk." Now I have been married long enough to know that there is not an option here. There is no "think". There was obviously something important going down. Besides I have also learned over the years that Karen has frustratingly good ideas. She has the gift of walking into an unknown-to-her situation, sizing it up, and making a suggestion as to how to do whatever-needs-to-be-done in a simpler and more elegant way than I have envisioned. She has saved me enormous amounts of work and time over the years. It is most frustrating. We sat down. Karen's basic idea was that together we would discuss the job at hand before work started – no more sneaky job starts saying "It will only take a moment". We would agree on an area of the boat that would be left untouched and the area would have to be large enough for Karen to sit and read a book. This area would be sacrosanct. No matter what happened, I could not encroach on this area without a job review with Karen. In this way,

Karen would have an area where she could work or just read, and could still be available for those times when more than two hands are required.

The suggestion worked. Karen was happy as she could remain on her boat. I was happy as I could work to my heart's content on the agreed-to job and mess the agreed-to area without feeling pressured. By this time, I had also learned to let Karen estimate the job time length and did not feel too badly when the job took much longer than I had originally estimated. And we both recognized the importance for Karen to always have a good book at hand.

A fiberglass boat is a scratch waiting to happen. The outside is all smooth and shiny but, behind those cupboards and lockers, it is a different world. The fiberglass on the inside of the boat is unfinished and has small, razor-sharp protrusions carefully placed to slice anything they come in contact with. Of course, all the boat plumbing and wiring run through those same areas. When I decided to replace all the plumbing, I did not know what I initiated. Hose does not like to be pushed around a bend, my arm does not reach under the settee, and the resistance of skin to those small fiberglass protrusions is zero. When I went on board *Vagus* in the spring to start working on the spring list, so too, went a box of bandages. The bandages were carefully placed within reach, not behind any doors that required time or a hand to open - the spare hand was usually too busy trying to staunch the flow of blood. The worst part of working in the spring was the cold. The combination of the scalpel-like sharpness of the protrusions and the cold weather, coupled with the fact that my hand was going where no hand had gone since the boat was assembled, made it difficult to notice when I was cut. I would normally find myself merrily working away and, suddenly, come across dark spots on the cabin sole, or on the fiberglass deck, or a smear on a cupboard. This initiated a frantic search of my various body parts, looking for the origin of the blood while simultaneously grabbing an oily rag or used tissue and heading for the bandage supply. I would return home with bandages stuck to various parts of my hands. After the first year, Karen quit asking what happened. She just had the disinfectant and antibiotic cream ready for me when I returned.

Karen became very relaxed about my infatuation with bandages and accepted the cuts as a normal part of doing boat jobs. "The job's not done until there's blood on the sole," she thought. This conditioning stood her in good stead one day when I installed the Ham radio. As part of the grounding system for the Ham radio, I needed to lay copper foil along the hull in an area under the cockpit and behind the quarter berth. To get to this area, I had to remove all the things stored in the quarter berth, a space that had taken on all the characteristics of a garage that one can no longer drive a car into. I then had to remove the paneling at the back of the quarter berth. This allowed a small opening into an area under the cockpit, the optimum area for laying the copper foil. The opening, not surprisingly, was just smaller than my shoulder width. To get far enough into this area, I had to lie on my side, stretch my arms over my head and wiggle myself carefully through the opening and around the engine controls. Both arms, head and shoulders were now in this enclosure. I could not move my arms down. I could only work with my hands to lay the copper foil – a strip about 50mm wide and a mm thick with a nice sharp edge. I had almost got the job finished. Just one corner needed adjustment, one bend too far. The sharp foil edge neatly sliced into my index finger. It was a good slice. I have experience with slices and I know a good slice when I feel one. Blood quickly came, dripping steadily on the copper foil. I had no tissues. Even if I did, my arms were extended over my head and I could only move my hands. I could not do anything to staunch the flow. I also realized I needed to get something to stop the flow before moving too far or I would have a major cleanup job later. Fortunately Karen was close by. She was quietly reading in her allotted space, which happened to be the port cockpit seat. She was not far away physically but she was far away for sound to travel. I did not have time for a long explanation. My lifeblood was steadily dripping away. I needed help, and help fast, with not a lot of questions. So with the clarity of one very concerned about oneself, I called out, "Blood! Blood!"

Karen immediately jumped to action thinking "He has done it now, there must be blood everywhere!" She sprang down the companionway stairs, grabbed some paper towels, and passed them up to me in the quarter berth to wrap around the finger. She then went for the bandages, passed a couple to me, stated she was in a good part of her book and returned to her reading spot. "Jim certainly knows how to bond with his boat," she thought.

# 3. *Slip Sliding Away*

*I* stood, stretched, poked my head over the dodger, felt the breeze embracing my face, and scanned the horizon. Still nothing. My shift was nearly over. I powered up the radar and checked for boats. Several freighters showed up about twelve miles out. We were approaching the shipping channels – just in time for Karen's shift. I always did have good timing. With a little time left, I settled back and thought back to when we left this summer.

We had set a date - actually, several dates. The first was when we would leave our home marina at La Salle Park. We had been discussing possible dates with our friends, Daryl and Ann, over the winter and decided it would be fun to travel with them down the lake at the start of their summer vacation. Daryl and Ann always started their vacation on the first week in July. In February, this date had looked good and we thought there would be lots of time to get ready – or at least we hoped. During the last season, we had watched other couples, going on a similar trip, working on their boats until the last possible minute. It was well into the fall and the docks were ready to come out for the winter before these sailors left on a rushed, cool trip south. We wanted to have a more relaxed, leisurely time of it and be able to stop and "smell the roses" along the way. A July leaving felt good. We would cruise Lake Ontario for a month to sort out the boat systems, then head south in early August. There should be plenty of time to stop along the way, as the only target date was the boat show in Annapolis in mid-October. A plan was made. We would retire in April and then devote the next few months to all the last minute items and boat chores to get ready to go. March was spent in a flurry of list making, editing and prioritizing.

It was a clear sunny day in April; one of those beautiful days that occur in Southern Ontario after the dreary days of March; a day after the long days of winter that one just wants to breath in and absorb. I was driving home from my last day of work. I shoved in an Alabama CD and played "I'm in a Hurry To Get Things Done". I sang along with the music; I can sing quite well in the car as long as no one is with me. Singing along with the music, I remember thinking, "I'm in a hurry to get things done – NOT!" I was wrong of course. It was 2:30pm. I felt slightly guilty at leaving early, but no one expected me to return after the good-bye luncheon. My work buddies were returning to their lives and I was moving onto something else, something quite foreign to most people. I had spent the last few days saying goodbye to a lot of people. People I had known, worked with and had fun with, some for over thirty years. I knew what I did at work, at least some of the time. In many ways, the workplace defined who I was. It was strange as it was a Monday. I did not have to travel this roadway tomorrow - or for a whole bunch of tomorrows for that matter. I would be traveling along a less defined path, a more fluid path so to speak. Driving down the road, I felt an odd mix of joyful anticipation at new things and unknowns in the horizon, and reluctance at leaving the security of work and friends behind. I wanted the drive to last for a long time. I wanted to remember this sensation. I did not realize I had just taken one of the first steps of leaving.

Armed with my finely tuned lists, I could now tackle all those boat jobs; the jobs that were on the "Absolutely-Must-Do" list. I soon discovered that the sad thing about a boat job list is that it does not get shorter with time. Just as I finished one job, a new job would appear to be added to the list. Sometimes more than one new job. As the July departure loomed, the "Must-Do" list was revised to a "What-Do-I-Have-To-Do-To-Leave-The-Dock" list. The time went quickly. I was so busy I wondered how I ever had time to work on the boat before I retired. The days got longer and the time grew shorter. All of a sudden, it seemed, we were giving our condo a final clean, covering the furniture, storing our car and moving aboard the boat full time. We had two days to spare. We had made it. Yes, there were still jobs - but there are always jobs on a sailboat. We were ready to go cruising. We had made arrangements to see our boys, Alex and Jeff, and daughter-in-law, Caitilin, in August before we left for the U.S. We said goodbye to people at the marina and, on a bright Saturday morning, left our dock for the last time, heading down the lake with Daryl and Ann. We had made another leaving.

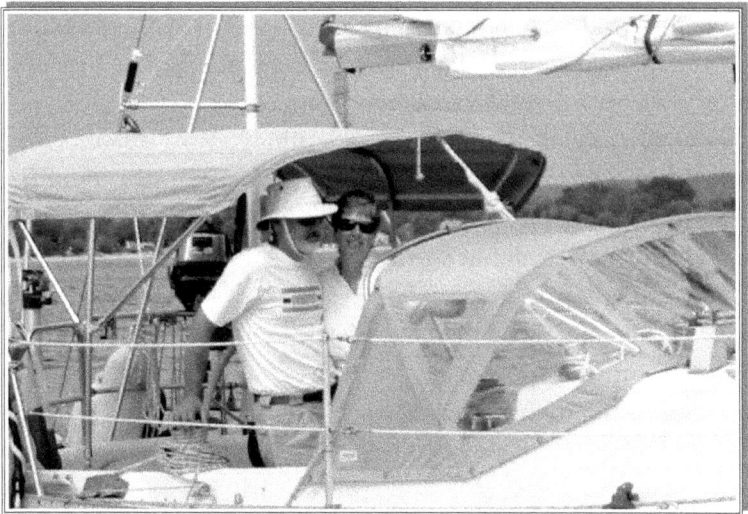

*Leaving*

Our first week went past like a normal summer boating vacation. We slowly made our way along the north shore of Lake Ontario in company with *Galadriel*, making sure that *Vagus* reached each destination first – after all, *Vagus* was the bigger boat. We did a few boat jobs, but mostly just enjoyed the time together with Daryl and Ann. We arrived in Cobourg to visit our mutual friends, Bob and Sue, on Canada Day. The six of us sat in *Vagus*, catching up on news and toasting Canada as fireworks burst beside Cobourg Marina. The next day was Bob's birthday and we gathered once more to enjoy each other's company. No fireworks for Bob's birthday - at least none we knew of - just a good time.

Too soon, the visit was over. We carried on with Daryl and Ann to Belleville, stopping for the night at the concrete entrance wall to the Murray Canal. It was a great place to overnight except for the mosquitoes that found a weakness in our defense system. About 12:30am, we could be found aboard *Vagus* plugging gaps and conducting mosquito search-and-destroy missions. After the first week, Daryl and Ann had to start their return to the land of the working. We were up at 6:30am, using our new alarm clock for the first time, to see them off. We reached *Galadriel* just as Ann untied the last of the lines from the dock. We said quick good-byes. How else does one say goodbye to good friends? We waved as *Galadriel* swung around in the channel and headed out of the marina. It was sad to see them go. We turned to walk back to *Vagus*. Now we were alone. We were together full time. We had said goodbye to our friends. It was another time of leaving.

The first week had been pure holiday, but now there were boat jobs to be done and new systems to try out and to become familiar with. This was the start of our new life as full-time, live-aboard cruisers. We could see how we enjoyed life afloat, while still in familiar surroundings, and practice our cruising skills. It was also a time to recharge our batteries before tackling the challenges that we knew were ahead of us.

Before leaving Burlington, we had traded our smaller inflatable dinghy and motor for a new Avon 3.1 meter inflatable, with an 8 Hp motor. We could easily plane with this dinghy, an important feature when moving about an anchorage in the Bahamas, according to the cruising books. "The distances are long and one has to be able to move quickly," the books stated. In our old dinghy we were only able to plow through the water at slower-than-sailboat speeds.

In July, the weather turned hot and humid. We were docked at a marina in Collins Bay.
"Why don't we go for a swim?" suggested Karen eagerly after lunch, just as I settled myself in the cockpit for a good read. "We can take the

dinghy out to the park by the entrance and swim off the dinghy."

"Why not?" I responded, putting down my book and sitting up. I recognized it was not really a suggestion. It was hot, however, and a swim did sound good. We motored out to the waters off the park, dropped the dinghy anchor and jumped in the water. It was the first swim of the season and it felt good. The clear, warm water in the bay felt refreshing on the muggy afternoon. While happily frolicking around the dinghy, we noticed clouds starting to gather, looking like a precursor to a Southern Ontario afternoon thunderstorm. It was time to get back in the dinghy and back to *Vagus*.

We knew that the "getting back in part" would be easier said than done. The old dinghy was hard enough to get into, but the new one had larger diameter side tubes. The difficulty level had escalated. In preparation, Karen, who had worried about this very problem over the winter, had purchased a dinghy step at the Annapolis boat show the previous fall. The step was a small plastic board, like a swing seat, with lines and hooks that were supposed to fasten on to the grab ropes along the dinghy sides. I had carefully hooked it on before jumping in. I tried it first. I carefully put my foot on the step while grabbing the ropes along the dinghy tubes. As I put my weight on the step, the step swung under the dinghy, taking my foot with it. I was left lying in the water, mostly under the dinghy, looking up at the darkening sky. Karen laughed so hard she couldn't tell the lake water from the tears in her eyes. We needed a better system. We tried using lines to haul ourselves aboard. We tried climbing on the motor. Nothing worked. Finally, after a few tries, I managed to power myself over the dinghy side, landing face first on the dinghy floor like a beached whale. Karen was still laughing but, at least, I was now aboard. Karen tried the power method as I coached. As she tried to propel her body over the tube, I grabbed hold of her bathing suit and pulled. "Let go!" shrieked Karen as she slid back in, pulling at her now thong-like one-piece suit.

She tried again to get aboard by grabbing my hand – I was not to touch her suit. She slid back. Karen did not have the upper body strength to make it into the dinghy using my technique and she was getting tired. I thought I would have to tow her back to the marina.

Then I had an idea.

"You rest for a moment and I'll get back in the water," said I.

"And what do you plan to do?" Karen asked suspiciously. She was learning about my ideas. I had jumped in the water by this time. Too much thought was not good for this idea. I got alongside the dinghy tube. "Come beside me and get ready to power yourself in," I said. "I'll hold onto to the dinghy and give you a boost to help you over."

"How are you going to do that?" she inquired.

"Don't worry, I've got it all figured out," I stated confidently. "It should be no problem. You can do this or I can tow you in."

Karen definitely didn't like the thought of being towed to the marina past all the other boats. She was not sure she liked what I was proposing either, but decided to give it a try. She got beside me and grabbed the ropes on the dinghy. She bounced up and down getting ready for one big heave. On the count of three, she kicked and pulled herself up with all her strength. I carefully placed my hand and shoved. Karen squealed, arched forward, and flopped gracelessly into the inflatable. She made it, thankful no one was taking movies! This skill we definitely had to work on.

Anchoring was another one of those skills where we needed to develop confidence. Most of our sailing had been in the western Lake Ontario region where one sailed from marina to marina. There were very few places to practice anchoring. We headed to Waupoos, a favourite spot we had discovered a few years before. There were only a few boats widely scattered in the anchorage. We found a clear spot, opposite a marina, and tucked in behind a tree-lined island. I watched the anchor settle in the clear water to the muddy bottom. After firmly setting the anchor, we could relax. The holding appeared to be good. It had been a long day and, after dinner and a movie, it was time for bed. It felt good lying in bed, feeling the gentle motion of the boat and listening to the wind playing in the rigging. Soon we were asleep.

The next day, high winds were predicted so I got out the Spade anchor. I had bought an aluminum spade anchor as our second anchor after much winter research. It was the latest technology in anchors and supposed to out-hold anything else, at least according to the reviews. I had to order the anchor from an importer in the States. As I pulled the anchor out of the locker I remembered back to a cold, snowy February day. Karen had called me at work to tell me that the postman had just delivered an anchor, all wrapped in cellophane, to our condo. The postman said that he had to deliver the parcel in person as they had bets on what it was back at the station. Now I was using the anchor. I was starting to feel like a real cruiser. I loaded the anchor into the dinghy and led the anchor rode from *Vagus* to a spot where the anchor would hold in the predicted wind shift direction. When listening to the weather reports, I had heard two different weather forecasts: one from Kingston and the other covering Lake Ontario East. Each forecast called for a different wind shift direction. I was learning about weather forecasts. Later that night, the winds hit and shifted in one of the predicted directions – fortunately, the direction the Spade anchor was set. I got up to keep anchor watch. "The first of many," I thought. Soon I read wind speeds of 20-25 knots with occasional gusts to 30 on the anemometer. The boat swung and the Spade anchor rode stretched out tight. The anchor held and all was right with the world.

The weather forecast called for another front to come in a few days. So far, the summer had been wet and windy. We decided that Kingston would be good place to visit until the weather improved. We had not been to the city in six years. Unfortunately, we picked Kingston's busiest weekend of the season. Kingston was hosting the Busker's Festival and boats filled the marina at Confederation Basin. Luckily, we found a spot on the day docks and were allowed to stay. We had a great time exploring Kingston by foot. There is something about coming into a city by water and having to explore by foot. One sees a different flavour than if one just drives in. The busker's were good and there seemed to be an act on every street corner and in every park. Kingston has an excellent downtown area to wander about, including a farmer's market within a block of the marina. The front came through, as predicted, and it was vicious. White caps formed in the basin and boats could not leave the harbour for three days. It was definitely a good time to stay and see the sights.

Finally, the winds began blowing in the direction that we wanted to go. This phenomenon is known in sailing circles as "favourable winds". Winds blowing from a sailor's destination make for a bouncy wet sail and are "unfavourable" or simply "bad". We were starting to feel the freedom of not having to go to work on Monday and, as nothing changes like the weather, we could now be somewhat fussy and wait for favourable winds to arrive.

Deciding to leave Kingston was one small, but important step, in the process of actually leaving. First, we had to shower. We never passed up an opportunity to use someone else's hot running water. Reaching the showers, however, involved a ten-minute walk through a hotel parking lot, down a street, around a corner, and down some stairs into a basement by the Marina office. After showering, there was breakfast, then cleaning up after breakfast. Then we had to walk into town to pick up the frozen meat that we had ordered the day before. The butcher, of course, didn't open till 10:00am. We needed to fill *Vagus'* tanks with water, as we had been staying on the day docks where there were no services. *Vagus* carries 80 gallons of water that normally last from 2 to 4 weeks, depending on how clean we feel we need to be. The marina staff was very accommodating and allowed us to tie up for a short while at a regular dock to take on water at no charge. Finally, with full water tanks, we headed to Portsmouth Harbour to top up the diesel tank and pump out the holding tank. Of course, several boats were already lined up for the diesel station and the pump out was the slowest I have ever seen - there is nothing like extending a yucky job. After going steadily for over four hours, we were cleaned, fed, watered, fueled and pumped out, ready to head for Gananoque and the Thousand Islands. This process is called "staging" in the cruising books. We were learning that it took time to leave. One did not just hop in the car and start the engine. Proper cruisers get ready to leave the day before they have to go. We were beginning to see why.

We sailed down past Howe Island, enjoying a nice lunch along the way - it was now well past noon - and entered a channel by Aubrey

Island into a very busy Thousand Islands. We had forgotten how busy this area could be and it came as a bit of a shock after being at the relatively secluded area around Waupoos. After checking a few full anchorages and a busy marina in Gananoque, we decided to head up the Bateau Channel to Trident Yacht Club. Trident was a great choice. They offered reciprocal privileges for the first night, and provided a remote, cottage-like setting. The dock we were given had a beautiful view facing the channel, and, while there, we were entertained by a blue heron fishing from the next dock. However, we were tired - it had been a long day. We were learning that there is no such thing as a rigid plan. Plans are just that ... plans. They could and should be changed depending on the times.

Eventually, we decided to return to Waupoos. For several windy days, we remained at the anchorage. Boat jobs got done, I played with the radar, and we took the dinghy to Waupoos Marina for ice cream and a paper. The Marina did not have any papers for sale but had one available for all to read – an Ottawa Citizen. On Saturday, the winds started picking up and gale warnings were out for the next morning. Waves were building in the anchorage causing *Vagus* to bounce to such a degree that we could not read. We tried playing cards in the cockpit. We looked over at the marina. It sat in dead calm, sheltered from the prevailing Westerly wind while white caps danced on the water between the marina and *Vagus*. "Why are we doing this?" we wondered. Indeed, it was a good question. We were learning another good lesson ... when in doubt, move out. We raised anchor and headed across the channel to the Marina for some land time. The Waupoos Marina is a great spot, very friendly and helpful. It was hard to believe that the winds were so high just a short distance off the docks.

The next day, while walking the docks, we met another couple who had done a similar trip to the Caribbean a few years before. They had kept a fun web site about their trip which we had followed. I had been particularly impressed by their report of loading twenty-six cases of beer on a twenty-seven foot boat before leaving Florida for the Bahamas (where the beer is expensive).

"Where did you stow all that beer?" was the first question I asked.

They replied, "We get that question a lot." Learning from other cruisers is another important skill.

July drew to a close - time to go to Cobourg to begin our travels south. We felt as ready as we would ever be after a month on the Lake. We started out from Waupoos and had a classic Lake Ontario trip - motoring, then sailing, then motoring again as the wind changed speed and direction throughout the day. Arriving at Cobourg about 9:30pm, we booked into the marina. It was time to prepare to leave the familiar sailing grounds of Lake Ontario behind - another time of leaving.

Cobourg is a delightful town on Lake Ontario. Over our years of cruising Lake Ontario, we had fallen in love with the friendly people, excellent marina and the nearby restored downtown core. Our good friends, Bob and Sue, now lived there as well, so it was usually a "must stop" on the travels. Cobourg is also almost directly across the lake from Oswego, New York, the entrance to the Erie Canal system and points south. We had decided to make Cobourg our departure point from Canada and had arranged to meet Alex, Jeff and Caitilin, in Cobourg before leaving.

On the first Saturday in August, we were standing by our boat looking anxiously at the parking lot for arriving cars. The kids were to arrive that afternoon, stay overnight on the boat, and return home the next day. Clouds rolled overhead with the unhelpful promise of rain. Plastic awnings were already placed around the cockpit to keep out any possible showers. The boat interior had been rearranged to allow three more people to sleep below. This was not an easy feat with all the cruising paraphernalia already aboard. The weekend was all planned.

Finally the kids arrived to much rejoicing. The dinner and evening was fun - updates on activities given and stories told. On Sunday, a fine misty rain descended on the area. A rain that did not really soak through, just dampened one into discomfort. A feeling of impending departure had descended on the group. It was not really clear when we would see

Alex, Jeff, or Caitilin again. We knew the trip south, if everything went according to plan, would take almost a year. Beyond that, who knew? It was open-ended; there was no fixed time for return. No date to grasp onto and say confidently "We will see you then."

We all went for a walk in the drizzle. We bought ice cream cones at the local beach vendor, as that was something that one does when walking by the beach. I proudly pronounced that the sleeping arrangements worked out quite well and they could all visit us on the boat sometime. Alex, Jeff and Caitilin dutifully nodded their heads and individually thought that a hotel room sounded a lot better.

The time came for them to leave. Everyone knew the time approached but, as when a group is asked for volunteers, nobody wanted to make the first move. We looked at each other. The time was now. Bags were gathered. Holding hands, we walked them out to the car. Hugs and kisses and promises were given all around, and the kids quickly piled into the car. Windows down, they drove off into the drizzle waving. We waved back, holding onto each other, afraid to let go, tears forming in our eyes. As the car drove out of sight, we turned and hugged each other. Time slowed. Carefully, we retraced our steps to the boat and climbed aboard. The boat was quiet and damp. It had an empty feeling that we had not noticed before. We held each other wondering "Why are we doing this?" We had left.

# Canal, River, and Ocean

**Across Lake Ontario, through the Erie Canal System, and down the Hudson River**

# 4. Locks, Locks and More Locks

*A*t last we were motoring into the first lock after two very long days. In fact, it had felt like one long "forever" day since the Thursday morning when we had woken up in Cobourg. Southern Ontario had been under a large stationary low and the weather had not been pleasant - particularly not the type of weather conditions for a fun sail across the 77 miles of lake between Cobourg and Oswego. Every day we had been walking to the local library, connecting to the Internet and checking the weather to see if a break was coming. On this particular Thursday, we had risen early and decided to do a boat cleaning first. I washed the outside of the boat and Karen cleaned the teak on the inside. It was a busy day. About 3:00pm, we finally took a break for our walk to the library. Once there, as usual, we took different computers to do an individual interpretation of the weather report.

On the walk back to the boat, I asked, "Well, what do you think?"

"It looks good if we go tonight," Karen replied. "If we don't, we may be here for a lot longer."

Southern Ontario was now between two weather systems and there was a one-day window before the weather got nasty again. We decided to go. When we reached the boat, we went into frantic get-ready-to-cruise mode, putting gear away and stowing items for the passage. There was not going to be much wind so we would likely have to motor across, about a thirteen-hour trip. As we did not want to arrive in the dark, we had dinner, a little rest and left at 8:00pm. The trip across turned out to be a gentle motor. We were too excited to sleep as we were heading to new lands. Besides, we could sleep when we arrived. Right?

At 9:00am Friday morning, we arrived at Oswego, booked into the marina and arranged for the mast to be taken down the next day. The bridges over the canal system are low so, for the next part of the trip, it was necessary to remove the mast and store it on the deck of the boat. We then arranged for our U.S. Cruising Permit and went through immigration procedures, officially entering U.S. Territory. Finally, we returned to the boat, looking forward to sleeping off our overnight adventure. We had just gone below when there was a rap on the deck.

"The mast crew will be short handed on Saturday and would prefer to take down your mast this afternoon instead." Up we rose and spent the morning getting the mast ready for removal. It was getting hot. The temperature was over 30C and we had now been up for over thirty hours. That afternoon we moved the boat to the mast crane; the mast was lifted out, and was stored on deck. It was relatively easy to remove the mast but it was a big job to secure the mast to its supports. The marina crew allowed us to stay at the mast crane dock. It was now 8:00pm. It was getting dark. We had been up for over thirty-six hours. We were hot, sweaty and bone-tired. And the marina showers were out of order. But, on the bright side, there was a restaurant across the street. After a quick scrub on the boat, we were looking blearily at menus. Knowing we had to move the boat first thing in the morning to free the mast crane area, we were back on the boat and asleep within an hour of the meal. It had been a long day, one of the longest days of our sailing lives.

First thing in the morning, we headed for the fuel dock. After topping up the fuel tank I announced while leaving the fuel dock, "I'm heading for the first lock. Better get the fenders out."

"What do you mean?" exclaimed Karen, her brow developing deep furrows. "I'm not ready yet. I thought we were going tomorrow."

"Nope," said I, "today looks good and the lock is open. Besides, we can dock along the wall on the other side for free. Just put the fenders on the starboard side." ("I think," I whispered).

Karen's face screwed into a look between intense concentration and incipient panic as she ran around securing fenders. I did not really know if the boat would be tied on the starboard or the port side, but I did know it was important for Karen to have a job at that particular point in time. My heart beat loudly as we got the green light to motor into the lock. The lock gates opened wide. We looked at the ten-foot walls ahead of us. We were going into a huge, drippy wet, concrete box. I saw that we could tie up on either side. I hailed Karen, who was still getting the last fenders in place, that we would, in fact, tie up on the starboard side. Sometimes I just get lucky. If it was the other side I could imagine the headlines – "World Cruiser Bludgeoned by Bumper!" Thank goodness it was not to be - at least, not today.

I managed to stop the boat between two steel cables. According to the guidebooks, the locks use three different systems to secure the boats while they are either raised or lowered. One system uses a steel cable securely fastened at the top and bottom of the lock. A person at the bow wraps a line around one cable and a person at the stern wraps a line around the other cable. By maintaining tension on these lines, they keep the boat from swinging when water is let in or out. We had rehearsed this routine - at least in theory. I had gone over the routine with Karen and Karen had nodded "yes". I was not sure if Karen had nodded her head "yes" because she understood what I said or whether she just wanted me to finish talking, with the expectation of figuring it out when she really needed to. Anyway, as I stopped the boat along the wall, Karen leaned out with the boat hook, latched onto the cable, slipped a line around, and turned to see what I was doing. At that moment, I realized I should be doing something. Luckily the boat rotated so I could attach my line with an unconcerned air. "An unconcerned air is important for the skipper," I had read. "It instills a sense of confidence in the crew." Unless, of course, the crew has been married to the skipper for thirty years and was wondering what was taking him so long. The lock keeper looked down, saw we were in place and were ready. He started letting water in. We were amazed. Water gently rolled in as we inched our way up the wall. Suddenly it was over. The gates started to open, we were given the green light and we motored away. Our first lock was history. We had really started on the adventure. Everything was new from now on. We motored for about one hundred meters, found a nice wall to tie up to, and relaxed.

I turned to Karen and said, "Now that was not too bad." "Now that was not too bad " was the exact phrase that I had used when the nurse wheeled Karen into the recovery room after she had given birth to our first child. The nurse overheard the remark and berated me for five minutes while Karen smiled. I could not believe I had uttered those exact words but, like water going over a fall, once those words started tumbling out my mouth, I was committed. I went very quiet, waiting.

Karen, who had just finished tying up the boat, smiled, much to my relief, and said, "No, that was not too bad at all." Maybe we would make it after all.

Over the next ten days, we would go through thirty locks as we traveled 184 miles from Oswego to the Hudson River. We would rise 175 feet above Lake Ontario and then descend 420 feet to the Hudson. Our sailboat had morphed from thirty-six feet to fifty-four feet with nine feet of mast hanging over each end. There are a lot of expensive pieces at a mast end so life was a bit awkward negotiating the boat with these overhangs. I had hung a red life seat cushion over the aft end of the mast in the hope boats behind us would see the end and take heed. Nothing hit us so maybe it worked. The cushion also was a bit of a conversation piece. People would wander over when we were docked near a town and ask about the red cushion on the end. They would then ask why the stick was lying along the boat and where we were going. I found this neat. I had never been a conversation item before. Well, I probably had been but did not know about it. I enjoyed stopping and talking to these people, politely answering their questions and finding out about where they were from and what they were doing walking along the canal. We found Americans to be very polite and curious people, definitely not shy. In Canada, people would walk along beside the boat, peering intently in. A boat, especially a sailboat with all the lines and rigging, is a mysterious conveyance to many people. When I appeared, the Canadian gawkers would quickly look away and try to look politely uninterested. Americans, on the other hand, would spot us, walk right over and ask what we were doing. I liked the attention. I was in the spotlight and I had an interesting story to tell. We were doing something that was different.

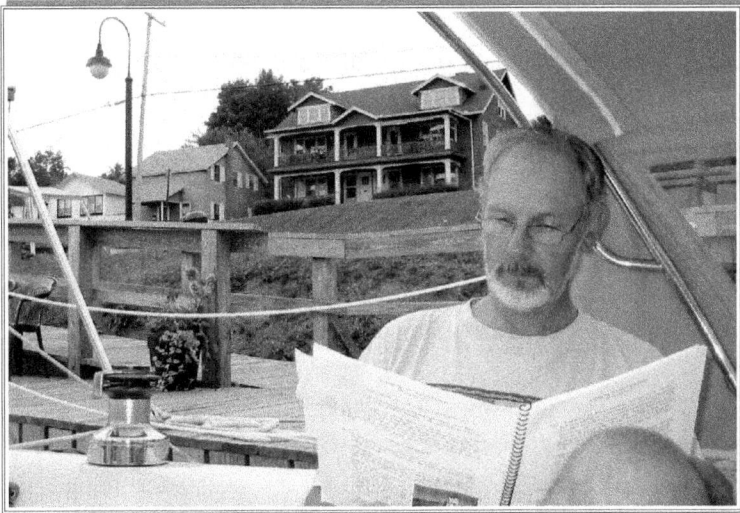

*Studying navigation for next day*

We soon became experts at "doing the locks". We actually started to relax and enjoy the experience. We worked as a team and had procedures down for hanging onto the various lock attachment systems. For the cables, we hooked on bow and stern. For the lines, we held on bow and stern as the lines were not attached to the bottom of the lock, but hung free. We actually found the line system to be the best for a sailboat. The hardest were the pipes. The pipes were widely spaced so we had to place a pipe at the midpoint of the boat. A line was then led from the bow and from the stern around the pipe. I would hold these lines at the midpoint of the boat, adjusting tension on the bow or stern line to keep the ends of the boat and, particularly, the overhanging mast, from swinging into the wall as water flowed into the lock. Karen, armed with a boat hook, would go to either the bow or the stern to help fend off and control the swing. However, a sailboat's sides are curved, not straight like a powerboat. This feature is great when sailing, but not great while going through a lock. The powerboats would go into a lock with pipes, tie off, and the flat sides would keep the boat from swinging -

piece of cake.  The sailboat would swing about the boat's midpoint, either going bow-in or stern-in, depending on which side of the lock the water came in.  One did not know this in advance.  Karen's job was to move to either the bow or the stern and fend off, usually a critical procedure during the sudden onrush of water when the lock just started to fill.  She learned to position herself at the boat midpoint, wait for a swing, then rush to the appropriate end to fend off.  Sometimes the end changed and she would rush to the other end.  If I was lucky, the end would change several times and I had the joy of watching Karen scamper up and down the boat, dodging all the lines holding the mast in place, boat hook in hand, usually muttering that she was not having fun.  I learned to be very quiet during those times.

One of the great features of the canal system was the free overnight tie-up  spots. After purchasing a ten day pass for only $37.50, we could use any of these overnight spots.  The tie up spots were numerous and well cared for by the lock keepers.  This gave us the chance to take our time traveling the canal system and to enjoy one of the other great features of this new lifestyle - meeting other people on boats.  After tying up at a spot, we would often walk around, saying "Hi" to the other boats or helping later arrivals dock.  The defining rule seemed to be that if one had seen the same boat at another dock, we had become old acquaintances.  It was just friendly to stop by and ask how their trip was going.  Soon little flotillas of boats with like speeds and traveling at similar paces would form.  These flotillas were loosely arranged with boats dropping out, new additions coming in or previous boats catching up, depending on the needs of the different cruisers.  People would stop to explore, to rest, to get groceries or just because.  Most of these people were doing what we were doing, taking their boat south, at least to Florida.  We had never met so many people doing the same thing.  It became an enjoyable time of comparing boats, equipment, provisions and plans.  Friendships were made and plans to keep in touch were formed.  It was a wonderful start.

About half way along, I decided the time had come for a nice, romantic evening by ourselves.  While traveling with people was fun, we also needed our time alone. Late that afternoon, I mentioned to the lock keeper that I was looking for a spot nearby that we could tie up for the night. The keeper suggested the wall beside the maintenance area near Fonda, New York, about 2 miles down the canal. The place was closed, as it was Saturday, and fairly isolated, but a good spot for the night. So we had a destination. We headed down the canal and spotted the dock, better described as a wall, on the other side of the canal. There were maintenance buildings in the distance but the area by the wall was nicely grass covered. There was not another boat around. In fact, except for the bridge across the canal about a half a mile away, there appeared to be nothing - nothing except an old large sign on the other side of the road leading to the bridge, advertising a fair ground. I swung the boat around and headed for the wall. The top of the wall turned out to be about three feet above the deck of *Vagus*, a fact difficult to judge from the other side of the canal. Karen, up to the task, scrambled off the boat, shorelines in hand. Soon we were secure. It was a warm, sunny evening. I could smell the grass in the field beside the boat. Wildflowers abounded. Karen started dinner and I opened a bottle of wine. We toasted our trip so far and this beautiful spot as we sat down to eat in the cockpit. The day's accomplishments were still fresh in our mind. The warmth of the evening enveloped us. Dusk came as we were taking the last bites of our dinner. Suddenly, lights flared all over the fairground and the valley filled with the roar of many un-muffled engines. The sound bounced off the valley walls before radiating into space. Each bounce reverberated through the boat cabin. What we initially thought were airplane engines were, in fact, stock car engines. We had arrived at the home of the Saturday night stock car races in Fonda, New York. With the thunder of cars racing around the oval, conversation became impossible. With no words we retreated below to the cabin, took out our books and read until the races finally ended at midnight. Nice romantic evening.

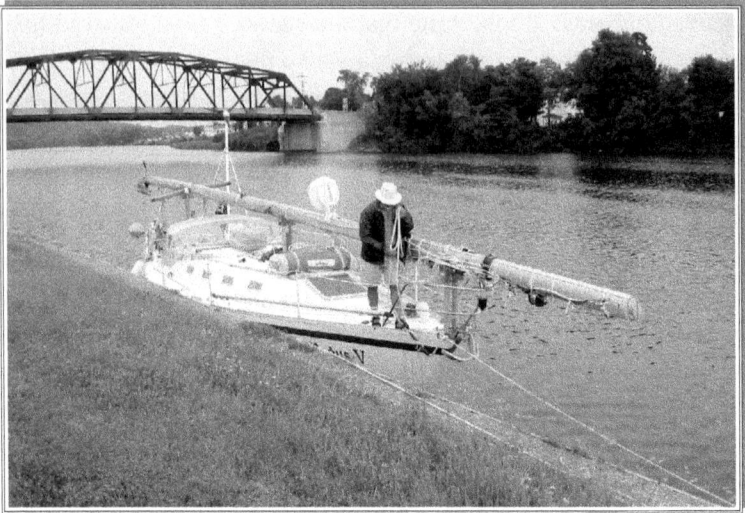

*Tying up at Fonda, NY*

On our tenth day in the canal system, we reached Waterford, New York. Waterford marks the end of the canal and the start of the Hudson River. Waterford also offered free docking for three days, shower facilities, a wonderful greeting party led by the Ladies Auxiliary and a great supermarket nearby. The supermarket even had a supply of grocery carts available at the dock for the cruisers to use. We found the last empty dock space and pulled in. First order of business was showers. This was the first shower facility that we had come across since leaving Oswego. It had been hot. We had learned about what were called "navy showers" aboard our boat and had been working out a showering methodology that used as little water as possible. To have an unlimited supply of hot water was a luxury to be coveted. Life could be distilled to a simple shower. We were sure that the good people of Waterford also appreciated the benefit of having the cruisers shower before venturing through their fine city.

While at Waterford, we met Ken and Carol, friends that we had made during the trip along the canal. Ken was in his cockpit, pulling apart various engine parts. After greetings were shared, I made the fateful mistake of asking what Ken was doing.

"Well," said Ken, "with all the weeds we have been going through, I thought I would check the engine water pump impeller. And look! Three of the five vanes have broken off. It's a good thing that I checked it or our engine would have overheated on the Hudson."

I wished him well and wandered back to our boat. "I wonder how our engine impeller is?" I mused.

Mentioning this conversation to Karen, she immediately responded that I should check our impeller as well, having visions of being swept along the Hudson without an engine.

"Besides," she said, "I can go and visit Carol as Ken should be finished by now."

So I started into the task. It was a still, hot August day with not a whisper of wind at the dock. Any movement caused a sweat to break out. The air was so heavy I felt as if I had to force air into my lungs. Under these conditions, I contemplated my next move. Sailboats are put together by sadists. Nothing is easy to get at. They were obviously never designed to be worked on once they left the factory. Having replaced the impeller before, I knew what kind of job I was getting into. My stomach felt like it had been kicked. I really did not want to do this. I had hoped that Karen would talk me out of it. "Oh, it should be fine." was what I thought Karen should have said. She didn't and, worst of all, I knew she was right. I had to tackle the impeller. First I cleared out the dreaded quarter berth and removed an access panel. Next I moved to the starboard cockpit locker, emptied it, and remove its access panel as well. Now I was ready. I gathered my tools and a spare impeller. Stretching and twisting my body through the access panel in the quarter berth, I placed my feet into the starboard locker, bent my head over, and squeezed my shoulders into the next locker. I could then look at the water pump. The job next involved removing the little bolts holding on the impeller cover. These bolts were small. They would sort of get lost in a man's fingers. I would usually drop one in the bilge and I expected to again. I placed a paper towel under the pump hoping to deflect a falling bolt into the locker. I started to sweat heavily. Water droplets beaded on my forehead and found a path towards my nose. Soon I had a steady drip departing from the end of my nose at an alarming rate.

Getting the cover off, I was relieved to notice the paper towel trick worked. I pulled out the impeller, banging one knuckle on the fuel pump, necessitating a trip to the head to bandage the knuckle (I had forgotten to bring the bandages). Back in the locker, I looked in horror at the impeller. One vane was cracked and one vane was missing altogether. "There is nothing worse than a missing vane," I remembered the instructor saying during the diesel mechanic course. "You must account for all vanes. Otherwise part of a vane will be stuck in your cooling system and your engine will overheat – just when you need it the most," the instructor emphasized. With a panicky feeling forming in my chest, I wondered "Where is the other vane?" Of course I could not see directly into the water pump channels. I had to go by feel and a little dentist mirror. I also needed my reading glasses and a small flashlight to use the mirror. My glasses were slipping down my nose. I had one hand holding the light and the other with the mirror. I was hunched over and starting to cramp up. It was not going well. I decided to try feeling in the pipes connected to the pump. Suddenly, I felt something that should not be there. The hose stopped! Grabbing the mirror and light. I could just make out a piece of vane stuck at the top of the hose. Carefully, I got a small piece of wire, formed a hook on the end and went fishing. Normally I do not have the patience for fishing but sometimes one can get lucky. I got lucky. The vane popped out. It fit perfectly on the impeller. There were no more missing parts! I felt a rush of elation that only happens when one knows the worst is over. Replacing the new impeller and bolting on the cover, I then headed for the cockpit and started the engine to check the water flow. All looked good. Life was good. Ken and Carol stopped by. They had just showered. They looked cool. Ken asked how it was going and I proudly showed Ken the broken impeller. "I'm glad I checked!" I stated. It was time for another shower.

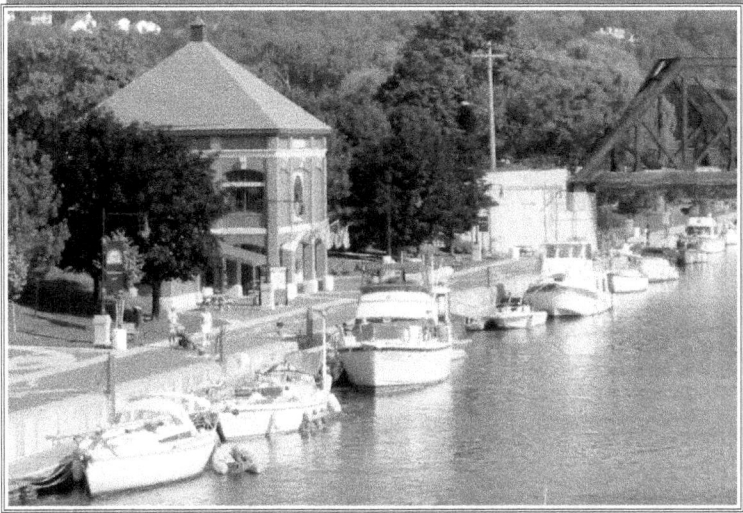

*Vagus in Waterford*

# 5. *The Cruising Permit*

*I* had read about officialdom when arriving in new countries. So far my only experience with this aspect of cruising had been when we had sailed across Lake Ontario to Wilson, New York. At that time, we were able to arrange for an I68 card ahead of time that basically provided all the information on the boat and crew. When we arrived in the U.S., I just called the number on display, provided arrival information and the I68 number, and presto! - Welcome to the United States! Simple. The I68 card was only good for limited stays, however, not the 6 months that we expected to be cruising U.S. Waters. For this trip, we would need a Cruising Permit. This permit gave permission for the visiting boat to cruise U.S. waters for up to a year and it was free. No other permits, decals, or documentation were necessary. One just applied for the permit at the first port of call. "Great," I thought, "this new port arrival stuff is a snap." I would be essentially wrong in every aspect of that thought.

When we arrived at Oswego, we saw signs in the marina office on how to apply for a Cruising Permit. I phoned the number and faxed the required information. So far so good. An hour later, I went back to the office and there was a fax copy of our permit. Our names and the boat name were handwritten on it. There was no document number on the form. A big stamp obliterated the initiating officer's signature, and our boat name was wrong. Thinking it unwise to travel around a foreign country with a permission form made out to a non-existent boat, I made another phone call. A blank form was again faxed and I filled in all the correct information. An hour later the duly stamped official form once appeared in the fax machine. We were ready to go.

The next day, as we filled the fuel tanks before entering the lock system, both a Customs and an Immigration official showed up at the marina office. I saw them and proudly announced that I had a Cruising Permit and had used the Immigration check-in with the new videophone. The officers, a bit surprised that someone volunteered to talk to them, turned out to be very pleasant and helpful. I confirmed that all *Vagus* needed was the Cruising Permit and that the I68 form and the boat decal I had needed in the past were not required. Being a "rules guy", I really wanted to be sure we were doing things correctly. I pushed it further. I asked about the need to check in when we moved from one district to another. There was some confusion about this procedure when I was researching the topic with other cruisers. After all, a car crossing the border doesn't need to keep checking in, why should a boat be any different? The officers confirmed that yes, we should check in and that the next check-in point would be when we reached the district of Albany. The officers apologized that they did not have the phone number for the various districts that we would pass through. The listing that they had was obsolete as they were in the middle of reorganizing under the Homeland Security banner. "Alright," I thought, "Albany it is."

We proceeded along the canals and onto the Hudson River. We got our mast re-stepped and headed down the Hudson towards New York. As we neared Albany, I remembered that I should check in. I collected the boat information, the Cruising Permit, and the cell phone and dialed the number. When the officer answered, I dutifully reported in as I was instructed to do, stating the boat name, that we had a Cruising Permit, and we were heading towards New York.

There was silence on the other end. "Could I have your I68 and decal number, please sir?"

I was surprised. "We were told that we don't need an I68 or a decal. All we need is a Cruising Permit."

"You're wrong, sir. You need an I68 and a decal. You need to proceed immediately to the nearest port of entry and get this documentation."

By this time feeling a bit frustrated, I started to read the information on the Cruising Permit back to the officer, information stating that all we really needed was said Cruising Permit.

"You are not listening, sir. You need an I68 card and a boat decal. You must check in every three days until you get this documentation. It is important that the government keep track of you in case anything happens."

I was by this time coming to the realization that Rule #1 in dealing with officialdom was "do not argue." I politely asked if we would have to check in every three days after we got an I68 card and a boat decal.

"No, of course not," said the official. "Then you will have all the proper documentation."

It was hard. I bit my lip, then my tongue. Karen quietly watched the veins on my forehead stand out. I did not say, "Then after we get the I68 it doesn't matter where we are if anything happens?" I instead said "Thank you, we will get an I68 and check in again in three days" "By the way," I asked innocently, "where can we obtain an I68?"

Silence on the other end, then a question. "Where are you?"

"At this time, we are anchored just outside Tarrytown, New York."

"Where is that?" said the official.

Now this stopped me dead in my tracks. My brain froze. I was talking to the Albany office. Albany was in New York. Tarrytown was in New York. Both were on the Hudson River. How should I answer? "Well, we are near New York, New York," I mumbled. "We will check in there when we arrive," thinking that we would be interned at Ellis Island shortly.

"Alright," said the official, "have a good day."

I had run head on into officialdom. Three days later, we were still in the Albany district. It was late on a Sunday afternoon and we had just finished anchoring the boat. I muttered to Karen that I better check in. I was not looking forward to it but I felt that it was a job that had to be done. So, taking several deep, calming breaths, I dialed the number. Another official answered. I dutifully explained that we had been told that we had to check in every three days because we only had a Cruising Permit and did not have an I68 card or boat decal.

Silence again on the other end. Finally the official asked, "Is that a new rule, sir?"

My brain again froze. I banged my head into the navigation table where I was seated. Karen got a worried look on her brow. Slowly I recovered and explained the history of events to the officer. The officer patiently listened and asked what our cruising plans were.

I explained our planned trip down the Hudson, through the Chesapeake and down the ICW to Florida.

"Well," said the officer, after patiently listening to the whole story, "it sounds like a great trip. You just go ahead and have fun and don't worry about checking in."

Relief flooded over me in waves. With shaking hands, I thanked the officer and dutifully recorded the conversation in our logbook.

The Cruising Permit would not surface again until Annapolis. While visiting the boat show, we met a couple from Nova Scotia whose boat was on a mooring near us. We got talking about the Cruising Permit. Their boat had been boarded by the Coast Guard in Maine for a routine inspection and they had gotten into trouble for not previously checking in. Since then they had checked in at all districts down the coast. My heart fell. I would have to deal with the Cruising Permit again. I discussed this with Karen. We had already been in Annapolis for ten days and, if we phoned in now, I knew the first question would be "When did you arrive?" I felt that answering "ten days ago" would be a bit awkward. We decided to check in at Norfolk, the entrance to the ICW. All boats had to go through Norfolk so they should be familiar with the Cruising Permit.

When we reached Norfolk I dialed the number, feeling a sense of impending doom  An official answered. She asked when we arrived. So far so good as we had only got in a couple of hours before. Next she asked for the Cruising Permit number. I explained that our form had no number. The official sighed. She then asked when we had last checked in. I did not expect this question. They knew! We were being watched! I blurted out the whole story from Oswego on. "Let them take me," I thought. Headlines read: "Canadian Cruisers Deported from Norfolk." Confessing was probably the best thing I could have done. The official understood, realizing that there was confusion about the check in procedure. She duly recorded our boat information and told me where the next spot to check in would be. We were done. We could now proudly say that we had checked in. Officials on the ICW understood about the Cruising Permit. Life was good again.

# 6. *Cruising Down the River*

*A*fter leaving Waterford, we were looking forward to getting *Vagus* back to looking like a sailboat. The long mast looked too much like a battering ram for our taste. It would be nice to have it once again vertical, rather than horizontal. We left the confines of the canals, venturing forth on the mighty Hudson River. We had never motored down a river before. Shortly after entering the river, we passed our first powerboat, the first of many to come. Powerboats travel faster than sailboats - in fact, they travel considerably faster. A characteristic of this rapid progress through the water is the phenomenon known as a "wake". We would get to know and understand wakes very well. Basically, a powerboat cuts a hole in the water and pushes out short, steep-sided waves - the wake. On a sailboat, one has to approach these waves very carefully, at the correct angle, to avoid rolling from side to side or being bounced up and down. The waves cannot be ignored.

What is the correct angle? I was pondering this very same question as we approached our first set of wakes on the Hudson. The mast was still tied down on the deck, as we had not yet reached the marina where we could have it raised. Normally a sailboat can happily take all sorts of different motions and waves being thrown at it. It's the people inside that usually complain. This is when the mast is in its proper place. The vertical mast, together with the sailboat keel extending beneath the hull, act like a tightrope walker's balancing bar, reducing the rolling motion. What happens when a tightrope walker tries to walk out with only half a bar held in one hand? The same thing happens to a sailboat without its mast up. It rolls. It rolls quickly and uncomfortably. I saw the waves coming. I gently turned the boat and told Karen to hang on. "Oops! Too much into the waves!" I thought - just as Karen said, "I thought you were supposed to take the waves at more of an angle?" The bow went up. The bow went down. The mast hanging off the end of the bow came down a fraction of a second later. The boat and mast were not in perfect harmony when we hit the next wave. I remembered reading that there was no other single item on a sailboat more expensive than a mast. Just as I began to fear the mast might become a sacrifice to the river, the waves diminished. The mast stayed on. I had a few more gray hairs. Karen now started to relay the proper technique for taking waves, based on her rowboat experience. I nodded agreeably. What could I say? I would have to get the next set right. I began to search for approaching powerboats, thinking how I would now take the proper evasive maneuvers.

At that moment Karen said, "There's a boat about to pass us from the stern." Sweat broke out on my brow. I had just figured out the proper techniques and approach angles for a bow assault. The powerboats must have known this. They were definitely after me. How do you take waves on the stern? It was too late to turn bow first into the waves. I tried to go with the waves. *Vagus* surged forward as the wave crest passed underneath. It was not too bad a motion, only we were now riding the waves towards the shore and all the hard parts that could hurt a boat. I tried turning the boat, taking the waves on the stern quarter. This approach started a rolling, twisting motion, sort of like a drunken sailor walking along a bouncing, floating dock. Everyone, including the mast, had to hold on firmly to avoid being thrown. It was definitely not comfortable. After that, Karen kept a sharp lookout behind me so we could slow down and turn into any passing powerboat wake. Finally, with a big sigh of relief, we turned into the creek where the marina with a mast crane was located. We thought that travel should be better with the mast up.

We left the marina on a Sunday, happy to be a real sailboat again. It was a beautiful day. The guidebooks clearly stated that weekend boat traffic on the river was heavy and travel should be avoided. However, it was such a beautiful day. We wanted to get going. What was a little boat traffic? The passing scenery was amazing as the river ran down valleys and through cuts between hills. We had never experienced this type of cruising before. Soon we learned the proper passing procedure when powerboats wanted to pass from astern. When the powerboat was near, I would slow *Vagus* right down. The powerboat did the same and, by nature of the fact that a sailboat's slow speed was slower than a powerboat's, the powerboat would slip by, hardly throwing any wake. It was starting to be fun again.

About a mile from a twist in the river around Westpoint Military College, I spotted some white water at the twist. It was just after lunch. Drawing closer, we realized that the white water came from a large number of powerboats and sea-dos. They were all heading our way, out for an afternoon ride, and they were all going full throttle. It looked like a race to the local picnic beach, a beach that appeared to be behind *Vagus*. I counted eleven powerboats of various shapes and sizes, and six sea-dos merrily jumping the wakes thrown up by the powerboats. Sea-dos like big wakes. I looked at Karen. Karen looked at me.

"Any suggestions?" I asked.

"Yeah, we had better hang on," replied Karen.

With hands tightly holding onto bolted down parts of the boat, I steered straight ahead to present a minimum target, hoping the powerboats would miss us. There was nowhere else to go. I tried to think what the proper rules of the road would be - we never had this situation taught in Power Squadron class. I could see it as an exam question. "What course does one steer when eleven power boats are fanned out across the channel and heading straight towards one?" Good luck. As the powerboats approached, they angled slightly away, like a parting of the sea. *Vagus* kept on a straight course down the middle of the river. The sea-dos naturally followed the powerboats so they did not present a problem. Waves came from every direction. Waves intersected, they canceled themselves out, and they combined together to form triangular mounds. There was no question about steering into the waves. Straight ahead was as good a direction as any. I thought that this must be what "confused seas" were like when the forecasters said to expect confused seas. With waves coming from so many directions, the ride was amazingly smooth, except for the odd loud slap as an errant wave banged against the hull. I felt that sense of elation that one only gets after having gone through a difficult situation and coming out unscathed at the other end. We looked at each other and laughed. We would remember this Sunday afternoon's trip.

Tides, currents, and sailing in salt water were all new to us. We knew in our heads about tides and currents but had never really come to grips with them. Our sailing had been on Lake Ontario, which is a fresh water lake with, of course, no tides or significant currents. The Hudson would indoctrinate us. Our first brush with tides came at Tarrytown, New York. Tarrytown had installed a dock at the local marina where one could pump out waste and take on fresh water. We decided to take advantage of this service one morning before heading to New York City. We arrived at Tarrytown and tied up at the dock. First order of business was pumping out the holding tank. The pump out was located just below the outdoor patio to the marina restaurant. The patrons were able to watch this less than pleasant activity, if they were so inclined, while sipping on a local brew. Fortunately, no one was on the patio when we arrived. We then started to fill our water tanks.

Karen is a worrier. She knows me. Realizing she had to be a full partner in this adventure, she had taken on the difficult task of being the official worrier for the voyage. Every couple needs one. Some share the job. However, with me, Karen knew that the worrier position was hers by acclamation. It is not in my nature. So on arrival, she got into her role and looked around for something to worry about. Part of her looking around involved checking the depth as we arrived. She knew the bottom shoaled towards shore and she also knew about tides. Initially, all looked good although the depth was only six feet. *Vagus* needs five feet of water before becoming officially aground. At least, I had told her that five feet was the magic number, and five feet was burned into her brain. The thought of the river bottom and the boat keel meeting did not amuse her. Her brow furled in concentration. There must be something that she had not thought of.

"Jim, how much will the boat go down in the water when the tanks are full?"

"About an inch," I replied, as I sat watching the water from the hose pour down the tank filling tube. Karen thought some more.

"When is low tide?" she asked.

"About 11:00am," I said.

It was 9:30am. Karen checked the depth sounder. It now read 5.6 feet. The tide was falling. She called out the drop. Now I started to worry. I knew enough to listen to the official worrier when she was onto something.

"Keep an eye on the depth sounder and tell me when it reaches 5.3 feet, and turn on the motor," I said. I kept filling the tank, willing the water to flow faster. This was the last chance to fill up until we were out of New York City. I moved the hose to start filling the other tank. It was getting towards 10:00. People were starting to gather on the patio. They thought they might be in time for a bit of entertainment. Going aground at the water dock must be a routine occurrence.

Karen called out, "5.1 feet!"

I had enough. "Shut off the water, Karen, and start untying the boat," bundling the hose as I spoke. I jumped into the cockpit and put the motor in reverse as Karen climbed aboard. The depth sounder read 5 feet. Slowly *Vagus* inched away. She felt like something had gripped onto her and was trying to keep her from moving, but move she did. The early morning diners turned away and went back to their paper and coffee. We had made it.

Karen, after putting away the dock lines and returning to the cockpit, asked, "Why did you leave it so late?"

Smiling confidently, " I allowed for an extra 2 tenths of a foot so we should be good to 4.8 feet, not 5 feet."

Karen glared, "Well, did you account for all the extra weight of our cruising equipment and supplies and full water tanks?"

I went silent. I knew what she was thinking.

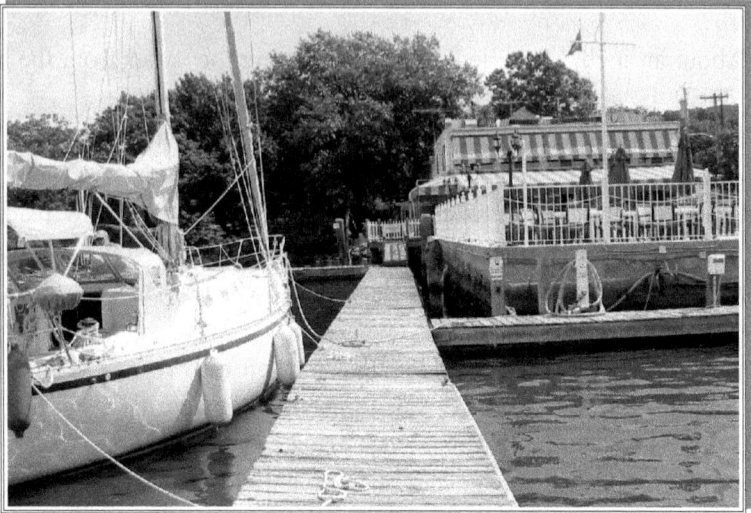

*Pumping out at Tarrytown, NY*

Tides were not the only item in our lesson plan. The trip down the Hudson River introduced us to the joy and the curse of currents as well. The joy consisted of going in our chosen direction with the current effortlessly boosting our speed over the ground. And the curse was driving into a current flowing against us. When the wind combined forces with the current, we would start to wonder if we would notice signs of aging by the time we got past a particular landmark.

*Vagus* also got to experience the feel of saltwater for the first time. Saltwater did not like to stay below the boat but had a wish to splash up on the boat deck. It especially liked to splash over the dodger hood and soak me when I was not looking. Even when I was looking, for that matter, it would splash me. It did not care. The saltwater would then dry and leave little salt crystals sprinkled over the deck. The boat became a regular salt factory. The crystals would grab onto our hands and feet, then leap off them, as we moved about the boat. During the night, the crystals would take any moisture in the air and form little wet spots on the floor and cupboards for Karen's morning entertainment. The war on salt had just begun. The salt also liked to deposit on *Vagus'* stainless steel. This steel had never seen a salty day before. It also was not prepared. I soon realized that the name "stainless" was appropriate as this type of steel only stains less than carbon steel.

There was a good thing about the salt water, however. The spiders left. Spiders were a fact of life while cruising Lake Ontario. They came in all sizes and hid carefully away during the day. They would then come out at dusk and spin beautiful webs around the boat. Karen had become expert at flicking spiders overboard just as they were about to drop from the bimini onto an unsuspecting guest's head. Spiders apparently did not like the saltwater. En mass they disappeared wherever spiders go when they want to get away. In some ways, we missed the spiders. Karen would often get a dreamy look in her eye at dusk while she glanced around the cockpit, her hand twitching.

# 7. *Waiting for Weather*

*V*agus sat nicely attached to a mooring at Atlantic Highland Yacht Club. We had sailed through New York harbour and down the South New Jersey shore to this spot. It was supposed to be a good place to wait for weather, whatever that meant. Actually, I had not thought about this stage of the trip. I had read and planned the trip through the canals. I had researched and knew the history of Chesapeake Bay. I had three annotated guide books dealing with the trip along the Intracoastal Waterway. Somehow I had blocked the part from New York to Chesapeake Bay from my mind. Whenever Karen had asked me about this part, I had casually said that we would "flit" down the coast into Delaware Bay, go up the bay to the C&D canal and along the canal to Chesapeake Bay. Karen would learn that when I became general, she had to get particular - for that was the length and depth of my plans for this stage. Now we needed to embark on our first offshore voyage on the mighty Atlantic Ocean. I had been so focused on the canals and the Hudson that this part was alien to me. I did not know where to start, but all the books said that one should "wait for weather" here, so "wait for weather" we would.

Confidently, for the skipper must always inspire confidence, I said, "We will take a break for a few days, explore the town, get some provisions, and plan the next phase of our trip while waiting for weather." It sounded good. I thought that it should give me time to develop a plan. Little did I know that we would have lots of time for a plan, as the ideal weather window occurred the day after we arrived and another would not happen for 10 days.

I hit the books. We had lots of books and guides. I looked at everything except the book on Chesapeake Bay. "Why would that book have anything on getting to the Chesapeake?" I thought. I was wrong of course. Later I would discover that that particular book had a very clearly written section on how to travel between New York and Chesapeake Bay, exactly what I was looking for. I got out the charts. I looked at the paper charts. I plotted courses on the electronic chart plotter. I calculated sailing times. Finally, I said to Karen that we had to talk. There were two fundamental strategies to get from Atlantic Harbour to Cape May, the entrance to the Delaware River. One involved two long day trips down the coast, first stopping in Atlantic City, then Cape May, and the other was doing an overnight trip down the coast directly to Cape May.

"You mean we have to go out on the Atlantic?" asked Karen. "I thought that you said we would be on inland water to Florida."

"Ah," said I, my brain working at a feverish rate. "I meant to say that we are going to be on inland waters except for this little bit where we have to "flit" down the coast." Quickly I grabbed the chart and, making little flitting noises, showed our potential routes.

Karen became serious. She had also taken all the navigation courses. She, in fact, could navigate as well as me.

"I want to look at this," she said, grabbing the charts and books. I decided that the stainless on the bow pulpit needed a really good polish.

Later that evening, Karen called me. "Those are pretty big "flits". And how do we know what a good weather window for this passage is? And do you know that a hurricane is making its way up the coast as we speak? What is our plan if it turns into New York?" she queried, calmly hitting all the critical issues before us.

Now she just had done something that gave me a great deal of difficulty. She had asked multiple questions. In fact, she had even almost exceeded my three capability. This was definitely serious. I never knew how to answer these multiple questions. Usually when Karen exceeded the one question level, I would just utter a random string of yes's and no's until Karen slowed down and repeated one question at a time. I did not think that this would be a good time to try this particular tactic. I tried to remember the questions.

"Yes, they are big flits. I don't know about a window. Yes, I know about the hurricane, but its' way offshore and I don't know what to do if it turns towards New York," I mumbled.

These were the answers Karen expected and was afraid of hearing. Her worry gene kicked into overdrive. She would have to get more involved.

"Well, we better start working on those answers, hadn't we?" she exclaimed, grabbing her book to settle for a calming read.

The next day was rainy. The good news was the hurricane was staying offshore. The bad news was large swells from the hurricane were expected to start hitting the coastline and it would take about three or four days for the swells to subside. As lake sailors, we had never experienced large swells. What did it mean? Could we safely sail in them? After all, the swells were supposed to have a long period so one should be able to go up and down them easily in a boat. The problem, according to the books, was not at sea but the ability to go into harbours. The swells would break at the harbour entrance making passage into or out of the harbour dangerous. In fact, the coast guard often closed the harbours when large swells were present. We had a lot of questions. We decided to get some provisions. "Going grocery shopping" in sailor talk is "getting provisions". I am not sure how the wording originated but it certainly sounds more exotic to go ashore to "get provisions" rather than "pickup bread and milk".

It was still raining when we decided to get provisions. With empty backpacks, we walked the mile to the store. On the way back, the rain came harder, the sort of rain that one might imagine was a precursor to the flood. We looked for shelter and spotted the yacht club clubhouse. It looked open. We made it to the front door and, dripping water, climbed the stairs to the bar. Several club members were also avoiding the rain before going to their boats. We were welcomed in.

"Ah ha!" I thought, "this should be a good spot for information." After the normal round of introductions, the members asked where we were going. "A great opening," thought I. Out flowed a series of questions about swells and weather windows and hurricane holes. We soon received the collective wisdom of the bar patrons. Many of the answers confirmed our own thoughts, which did not ease our minds. At least, we felt that we were on the right track. We learned that the harbours were dangerous when swells were forecast - great for surfers who flocked to the beaches but not for boats on the move. We learned that winds from the east and south should obviously be avoided but a strong west wind coming off the land could be fun when going down the coast. And we learned that we were not in a hurricane hole and really should have the boat hauled (difficult as everyone else would want to do the same), or find another spot, if a hurricane turned our way. We also discovered many of the bar patrons had no more experience sailing on the Atlantic than we had. Armed with this newfound knowledge, and bolstered by the generosity and friendship of the club members, we regrouped on *Vagus*. I got out the charts and checked the weather. The swells were still present and would be present through most of the week. However, a weather window appeared to be opening in about three days. We thought the swells should be lower by that time so decided to get ready to move.

One of the items on our get ready list was laundry. The next day also rained - when better to do laundry? We had found a large Laundromat in town. Carefully packing all the clothes for washing in a dry bag, we once again called for a pickup by the club tender and trudged through the rain. At the Laundromat, Karen came into her own, quickly surveying the facility and commandeering several machines. She then started the mysterious process, at least mysterious to me, of sorting the laundry. I could never quite see the sense or pattern to this sorting routine. As a result, quite fortunately for me, Karen would never let me do the laundry. I wandered to the grocery store to pick up more provisions, now we were looking at going, leaving Karen to complete the laundry.

When I returned, I found Karen in conversation with a French Canadian couple, J.P. and Colette. I was used to this happening. I would, in fact, be surprised if it did not happen. Left alone at a Laundromat, Karen would usually get to know the other people. We had actually made several very good friends that way. In fact, we met some of the nicest people at a Laundromat. J.P. and Colette were obviously cruisers. This was another thing that one soon learns to spot. Cruisers usually stand out in a crowd. They wear practical clothes, that are usually slightly rumpled. They also wear practical shoes. Ones that are good for walking and look like they have been wet and dried in the sun several times. Cruisers, as well, carry either large shoulder bags or a small backpack or both. J.P. and Colette had just arrived at the anchorage and stopped to do their laundry as well. Karen had spotted them coming in and had offered to show them the ropes - machines that were good and machines to avoid, hot dryers and cool dryers, where to get change and soap. In general, answering all those questions one would have when first entering a new Laundromat but would be afraid to ask. Karen knew Laundromats.

Introductions were made and backgrounds and plans exchanged in that wonderful experience while cruising called "meeting new people". Part way through the discussions, J.P. pulled out a small notebook and flipped through the pages to look up a certain part that he needed. I stared in amazement.

"Karen!" I exclaimed excitedly, "He has my notebook." Quickly, I reached into my backpack and pulled out my notebook. It was an exact copy of J.P.'s. It was the same manly colour and had the same dog-eared look from extensive use. J.P. and I looked at each other and laughed. We were friends. We had bonded over a notebook.

Colette rolled her eyes and asked Karen, "Does Jim makes lists and write everything in it as well?"

Karen and Colette left J.P. and me to compare our lists. This was the start of a wonderful friendship. We would share the first of many happy hours together that night, making plans and telling stories.

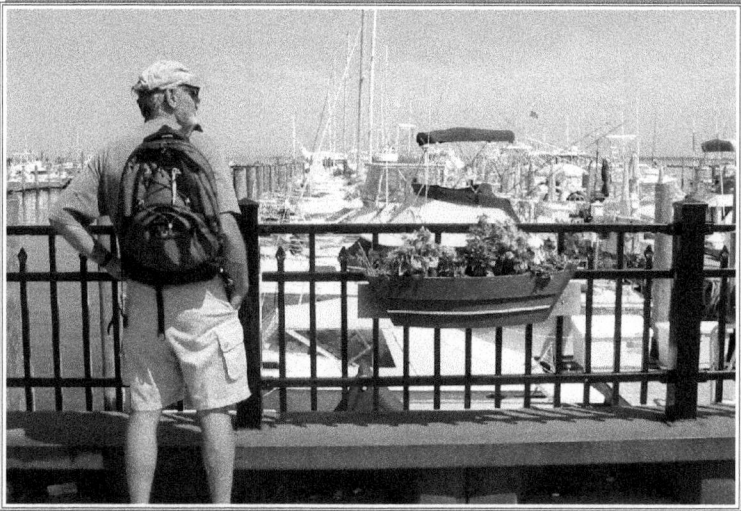

*Waiting for weather at Atlantic Highlands*

# 8. *In the Heat of the Night*

*W*e now had someone to discuss plans with. J.P. and Colette were also going to the Chesapeake and were concerned about the trip in the Atlantic along the New Jersey shoreline. And it looked like the elusive weather window was opening up. A two-day window of light, variable winds was coming, although the swells were still up. J.P. and Colette had also met several other boaters in the anchorage who were waiting for a good window. Along our travels, there were natural stopping places where the number of boats would build up, waiting for suitable weather for the next jump. This was such a place.

After further studying the weather and the charts, the weather looked good enough for an overnight trip down the coast, past Cape May, and into Breakwater Harbour on the south shore of the Delaware River. The swells thrown up by the hurricane offshore made going into any of the harbours along the coast not advisable. J.P. and Colette had come to the same conclusion. Upon discussing the weather window and the route, we discovered something else in common - we liked to make our own plans and travel our own route. While fun to travel together, as the voyage continued, we often would part, only to meet again in future days. J.P. and Colette checked with the other people in the anchorage and found that four boats were planning to leave on the same trip the next day. This gave us some encouragement, for we were either all very right, or all very wrong. "At least misery likes company," I thought. The group decided to leave the harbour at noon the next day and keep an informal radio check along the way. A noon departure should put us at Breakwater Harbour after dawn the following day.

At noon, we dropped the mooring line. Our first trip on the Atlantic Ocean had begun. We were excited. We were nervous. We would finally experience the mighty swells that we had wondered and worried about. We would have to go through all the marked off fishing zones on the charts. No one seemed to know what the zones really meant – does one go through the zones or avoid them? We would have to watch for all the night-fishing boats as well. It was new; another challenge, another adventure. We were ready. We had rigged the boat for sea - for heavy weather, actually. Everything had its place: tied down, bolted down, wedged, and secured. The ditch bag was handy. The "hot bunk" in the salon was made up for catching a little sleep along the way. We had discussed watches and had agreed to three-hour shifts. Three hours seemed long enough to be able to get some sleep or rest and not too long for the person on watch. We made sure the radar and chart plotter were both working. Our course was laid in. We took on water and fuel and, at noon, we fell in behind the five other boats that had gone through a similar exercise. Well actually, we knew that J.P. and Colette had gone through a similar exercise as J.P. and I had compared lists. The other boats, we were not sure of but every sailor probably has a similar routine or ritual to go through before a long passage.

The little convoy motored past Sandy Spit and turned the corner into the Atlantic Ocean, carefully following the buoys to avoid the shoals around the spit. It would not do to run aground at the start of the trip! Soon we were motoring in the Atlantic. We raised the mainsail. The wind truly was light and variable, too light for sailing. It would be a motor sail.

"That's alright. We can handle a nice gentle motor," I thought as I locked on the autopilot, set the course, and adjusted the speed to keep roughly with the other boats. The day was sunny and clear; the sea air smelled fresh and clean. We looked at each other and smiled. We were off on the next phase. We had followed the ritual of waiting for weather and had been blessed with a nice day that so far was not a taxing sail.

Through the day and into the night, we motored. The wind filled in a bit - of course right on the nose. To keep our speed up, and to keep on course, we decided to continue motor sailing. The mighty swells were quite enjoyable. By this time, the swells were down to between one to two meters high. They were of a long period though, so *Vagus* gently went up and down as the swells moved to the shoreline. It was like taking a gentle ride through a rolling countryside. Around midnight, while I was on watch, we were about four miles offshore as we passed by Atlantic City. It was an incredible sight. All the buildings were lit in different pastel colours. It looked like a fantasyland full of promise.

Standing watch at night is a magical time. The stars are dense and brilliant. There are so many; it is hard to see familiar constellations. The moon reflected gently off the swells, bathing the water and *Vagus* in its glow. I got out the binoculars to look at the moon more closely. Individual craters and features showed clearly. Somehow the time seemed to pass quickly. I was never sure where it went. I felt that I just got settled, checked our position and the radar, looked around a bit, and it was time to call Karen for her turn. Every once in awhile one of our buddy boats would call and break into my reverie. I found these calls jarring, breaking the flow of my thoughts. Thoughts that were like pleasant dreams, to be enjoyed at the time and not remembered later. It was a time to be alone with these thoughts. I did not enjoy these interruptions, but we were part of this loosely knit group and I felt had an obligation to respond. Off Cape May, two of the boats were running low on fuel. These boats checked with the Coast Guard, found the entrance was passable, and headed in. Four boats, including *Vagus* and *Safina* (J.P. and Colette's boat) were past Cape May by the time this change in plan was made. We decided to carry on to Cape Henlopen and Breakwater Harbour. We would meet the others later at Chesapeake City on the C&D canal.

Just before dawn, the wind freshened. I rolled out the Genoa and we were sailing. I shut the motor off and, after 16 hours of engine noise, the only sound came from the water gurgling along the hull. I looked around and saw another boat's lights. It looked like one of our group. I decided to call. It was J.P. and they were sailing as well. We had both decided at the same time to turn from "trawlers-on-a-stick" to sailboats. Now it was a race. We sped, neck-to-neck, across the Delaware entrance, making Breakwater Harbour about eight in the morning. One boat in our flotilla carried on up the Delaware and the fourth boat, a larger boat, had reached the anchorage first and was just getting ready to drop its hook.

"Are you sure this is the place?" asked George on *SeaWalk* over the radio. "There is not much here."

Not quite knowing where "here" exactly was, I called back. "We will be at the entrance in about half an hour and will see you there." Wherever "there" was.

J.P. won, but the race was close. *Safina* pulled into the harbour just ahead of *Vagus*. George on *SeaWalk* was correct. There was not much there. In fact, there was nothing there except a big breakwater. The harbour was a shelter for large ships to wait for favourable conditions before heading up the Delaware. At least the anchorage was large and the holding looked good. Although the problem with a big anchorage area where there is only one boat at anchor is that distances are deceiving. There are no good reference points. One does not want to anchor too close to the other boats. However, there is no point in anchoring across the harbour from them either. Often what looks like "too close" is, in fact, quite a dinghy ride away. We tried to figure out where to anchor. The first time we dropped anchor, it was too far away and we were affected by the current around the East entrance. Next we moved close to *Safina*. That seemed better; our anchor stuck and held firmly. We could relax. We had made it safely down the coast on our first Atlantic passage. J.P. and Colette waved to us. It was a great feeling. We went below for some sleep. "Tomorrow - the Delaware," we thought.

During the day, the wind steadily increased. We knew that our weather window was short but it closed faster than we anticipated. Instead of having two good days as forecast, we only got one. By late afternoon, the wind was blowing a steady 25 knots, gusting to 30, from the North, right at the breakwater. The people that built the breakwater obviously knew something. The breakwater protected us from the waves that built up in the bay behind us but *Vagus* still shuddered in the gusts.

Contrary to popular belief, sailboats are not quiet vessels. Yes, when underway and sailing, they are quieter than a powerboat. They are not quieter at a windy anchorage when the wind makes interesting, howling noises as it tries to go through the rigging. The wind does not like to be cut apart in this manner and makes its displeasure known. It was definitely too windy for us to launch our dinghy to visit other boats. We knew the wind would have more control of our dinghy than we would if we tried lifting it off the deck. But we could look out at the other boats and know we were not alone in this latest adventure. And we could talk over the radio to our newfound friends. The weather forecast did not sound good. The wind was to keep up for at least another day. However, we were secure. We would just have to wait it out.

Later that day, we had just settled into our cockpit seats with a nice rum and water with a twist of lime, our standard boat Happy Hour drink, when I noticed that *SeaWalk* looked farther away. Karen also looked. Yes, *SeaWalk* did look farther away. In fact, they appeared to be moving away. I got on the VHF and called *SeaWalk*.

"I think you are dragging," I said after I got hold of them.

George and Ann were below having dinner. Soon heads popped out of the companionway. They were dragging. They got the engine going, raised their anchor - by hand, as their windlass was broken - and motored forward to anchor again. We settled back into our seats.

I turned to Karen and said, "I would not like to raise that anchor by hand." The anchor was the same weight as *Vagus'* - 22 kilograms. With the chain attached, George would be pulling up nearly 50 kilograms, not a pleasant thought. *SeaWalk* motored up behind us, dropped their anchor, and started moving back. They kept moving back, and back, and back, as the anchor did not grab. They pulled the anchor up and tried again. Again it did not grab. J.P. and Colette were now watching the drama. The wind still blew hard and the forces made *SeaWalk* difficult to hold. J.P. suggested they use more chain when they dropped the anchor. They tried again and again. It did not hold. George was obviously getting tired pulling up the anchor. Ann was getting panicky trying to steer the boat and it was now starting to get dark. The wind, if anything, was increasing. Karen got on the VHF and told them if they could pick me up with their dinghy, I would try to help them. Karen had good ideas in my effective utilization.

"You know what to do," she said.

"Yes, but I am not an expert," said I, with a worried furrow on my brow as I looked out at the windswept water. "We do not have that much anchoring experience."

"You can at least help out," she said. "And you know they need to let out more chain."

Ann, seeing that George was tiring quickly, told Karen that they would be over. They motored near *Vagus*. With a great deal of difficulty George lowered their dinghy. It was conveniently on davits at the rear of the boat but was partly deflated. He resolutely motored over to pick me up. The wind howled. Spray blew over the dinghy tubes and I was soaked in a few minutes. Fortunately, Karen had made me wear a foul weather jacket and life vest. We reached *SeaWalk*. By this time, Ann was at the edge of panic and George was really exhausted.

"I hope my triple bypass keeps holding up," George stated as I climbed aboard. I gulped, reassured Ann, and laid out a plan of attack. I would direct Ann using hand signals to motor up beside *Safina* where J.P. had said the holding was good. Ann would try to hold the boat into the wind while George and I dropped the anchor. When the anchor was out, I would give her the signal to reduce power and let the wind slowly push us back until the anchor grabbed. Once the boat was stable, I would then give another signal to go in reverse to set the anchor. Ann understood.

Slowly we motored up beside, then well ahead of, *Safina*. I gave the signal to hold the boat into the wind and told George to let go the anchor and let out about 100 feet of chain. We were in 10 feet of water. George released the anchor. Over it went with a splash, taking the chain with it. Chain ran out of the locker like a frightened rabbit. It kept running.

"How do you stop it?" I asked.

George grabbed onto the chain. That was not the way to stop runaway chain! The chain quickly pulled George's hand into the anchor roller. I also grabbed the chain and pulled it around the defunct windlass Gypsy. Fortunately George was wearing heavy rubber gloves and could pull his hand from the chain roller with only a few scratches, leaving a glove embedded in the anchor roller. At least 100 feet of chain had been let out. I gave Ann the signal to reduce power. *SeaWalk* had a very high free board that quickly caught the wind. I was amazed at how fast the boat moved with no power on. No wonder they had problems holding her in this wind. George was exhausted and now it was rapidly getting dark. I watched as *SeaWalk* fell back and the chain started to straighten. Suddenly, the chain came out of the water and stretched out in front of the boat. The boat turned rapidly into the wind with the chain becoming taut as a bowstring. The boat stopped. I felt the chain and there was no vibration. The anchor appeared to be holding. George let out another 20 feet for good measure. Ann put the boat in reverse and, with the wind and motor, the chain went taut again. We did not move. We were holding. I waited a few more minutes. The boat appeared stable and riding well.

"I think you are set."

George brought me back to *Vagus*, thankful and relieved. I was relieved too. Somehow everything had worked. It was now dark. My unfinished drink still waited for me. Karen had been carefully watching and had a towel and change of clothes ready. She started on dinner as I, drink in hand, settled into the cockpit seat once again, listening to the wind, feeling a few muscles that I had not felt before. Our first day at Breakwater Harbour was nearly over.

The next day the winds did not diminish. They remained high and steady. At least all the boats were holding well but it was still too wild to go visiting. We would spend the day reading, preparing for our trip up the Delaware, and checking on the weather to look for a break. George managed to contact the other two boats that went into Cape May. They found the harbour rough from the wind and were also holed up, waiting for an opening. Karen did not like this forced idleness. It was not that she did not like being idle. It was just that she preferred it on her terms. She liked to be in control and this was, without a doubt, beyond her control. She started paying more attention to the weather reports.

"The wind seems to be decreasing," she suggested.

I replied, "I know that is what the forecast said, but it still looks pretty windy outside. It will take some time for the waves to decrease in size after the wind drops."

George called for morning and evening conference calls to discuss weather reports and strategies. Another short weather window for going up the river might occur in two days. This window was still pretty tentative, however, and it looked like it might only last a day. As Delaware Bay is relatively shallow and affected by tidal currents, our departure had to be timed to ride the incoming tide. Dangerous waves could form when the wind was against the tide. The guidebooks had cautioned that it could be rough on the Delaware and the bay was to be treated with respect. The three boats remained where they were.

The next morning Karen got up to listen to the 6:00am weather forecast. The forecaster said the wind was dropping, which was good news. In fact, it was supposed to be only 15 knots. She checked the tide table. We would be able to catch the incoming tide if we left within the next half-hour. Karen was tired of staying in the middle of nowhere. Excitedly, she woke me with her news. Now I am not a morning person. In my pre-retirement life, I normally had breakfast alone, as making conversation after just getting up is not my strong point. It takes at least until after the first cup of coffee for my brain to finally acknowledge that it is just starting to open for business: "Verbal inquiries of the morning variety may be made. Acknowledgments, however, may or may not be forth coming." When Karen tried to wake me with her good news, I was in a very deep sleep. After listening to the wind in the rigging for the past day, while maintaining an almost constant anchor watch, a slight decrease in the wind told my body that we had survived the worst, the boat held, and I could really relax. I had been very asleep when Karen sprang her good-news-and-plan-about-leaving-in-half-an-hour upon me. And she was excited.

"We could make it!" she proclaimed.

She asked me what I thought and told me to call the other boats. I looked at her. The only parts of my body acknowledging her presence were my eyelids. They fluttered open. I had no idea what she was saying but she seemed excited. Somewhere a male gene kicked in that said, "when a female is excited, something is happening, and you better do something." I had no idea what all this "something happening" was. My body sprang out of bed and headed to the navigation table. The navigation table was my sanctuary on the boat, my bolt-hole. I loved to sit at this table. I felt comfortable there. So, like a horse heading for the barn, my body took me to the navigation table. Once there, I had no idea what to do next. My brain was just starting to take input from my ears and Karen was still trying to tell me something. Something about me being useless first thing in the morning. That I already knew. There must be something else. More words filtered through.

"The weather has calmed and we need to leave," I thought I heard.

Leave! I could barely get up. More bits floated into my consciousness. I was to call the other boats and "tell them our plans."

I slowly picked up the radio microphone as I heard "If you do not hurry we will miss the tide and have to stay another day. Oh, why do I bother?" exclaimed Karen, now totally frustrated at my inability to grasp and act on a perfectly good plan.

She stomped off to the settee. Well, she did not actually stomp. The stomping sounds were filled in by my brain as her body language definitely conveyed that a stomping action would have occurred if we were not aboard a boat. She was also good at conveying a door slamming. I wondered how she did this, especially as we had no doors to slam.

My hand, guided by some unknown force, moved the microphone to my lips and I heard myself call George on *SeaWalk*.

"Looks like the wind is dropping and the tide is with us," said my disembodied voice. "What about leaving right now?"

There was a moment's silence on the other end. "Jim had seemed to be a reasonable sort," thought George. George finally responded that he thought tomorrow looked better and suggested I check the breakwater before venturing forth. I signed off and, glancing at Karen who was still seated at the settee reading furiously, headed up the companionway to the bow of the boat to look at the breakwater. By this time, my brain was starting to get up to speed. The wind had dropped. The breakwater was still there. But huge columns of spray were being flung in the air on the other side of the wall. The waves had not yet found out that the wind had dropped and were still trying furiously to get rid of this particular obstacle in their way. We would not be leaving that day.

Just as I turned to go in, J.P. and Colette shouted and pointed at the water. There were dolphins. These were the first dolphins that we saw and, being so, were special. Everyone talks of seeing dolphins; they show pictures of dolphins, but it is not like seeing them for yourself as they swim around your boat. They are magical creatures and I hoped they came to tell us that it would be alright to go tomorrow. At least that was what I told Karen, who suddenly felt very sorry for me, believing that I was really overtired and sent me back to bed.

All signs held for an early morning departure. The wind was still dropping but was expected to pick up later in the afternoon. The waves had finally got the message and decreased in size. By leaving about 6:00am, the little flotilla could run with the incoming tide all the way up the Delaware to the C&D canal and with the outgoing tide down the C&D Canal. All looked good and the three boats in Breakwater Harbour and the boats in Cape May left at first light. We threaded our way up the river. I kept an eye out for shoals and Karen, seated in the cockpit, chart in hand, carefully plotted our course, giving me a running commentary on what to expect next. We were working once again into a good team. The wind started to fill in after lunch but we were far enough up the river that we were protected by the banks from any serious wave action. The weather window was very small, only about half a day. But we made it. The current carried our boat quickly up the river. With great delight, we spotted the entrance to the C&D canal. The tide was just starting to change as we entered the canal and we rode the outgoing tide along the canal.

The plan was to stop at Chesapeake City, a harbour half way between the Chesapeake and the Delaware. *SeaWalk* was already there and their radio message was encouraging.

"There's lots of room!" they said. They proceeded to give instructions on how to enter, as the entrance had apparently partially shoaled over. We headed in, watching the depth sounder steadily decrease. With a little extra throttle, *Vagus* happily shot into the anchorage. We made it. The other boats were there. We had not been off the boat for over five days at this point. The weather was closing in with rain and high winds again in the forecast. But we were now at the entrance to Chesapeake Bay.

# The Bay

Overnight on the Atlantic, up the Delaware, through the C&D Canal, and down the Chesapeake

# 9. Crab Pot Bay

*R*aising anchor at Chesapeake City, we decided to get fuel before heading towards Georgetown, our next stop. We had motored a lot during last the week. The diesel jugs on *Vagus'* deck were empty and her main fuel tank was only half full. Just as we reached the anchorage exit, we slowed for a huge, sun-blocking car freighter on its way down the canal. It was big - awesomely big! The fuel dock, on the other side of the canal, was built around a bridge support. It was actually hard to tell where the marina and bridge support parted ways; they appeared to be one. The fuel dock ran parallel to the canal and the bridge support was directly ahead of the pump. This information would just be of general interest except that the tide was changing. It was slack tide as *Vagus* arrived at the fuel pump but we did not know that slack tide only lasted for a couple of minutes. As the fuel gently gurgled into *Vagus'* tank, I watched the water start to move. The tide was ebbing and the water, moving from the Delaware into the Chesapeake, was coming from astern. I noticed the concrete bridge abutment was directly in front of *Vagus*, exactly where the water would push her when the dock lines were untied. After filling the main tank, I started to fill the jerry jugs on the deck. I looked at the water as it began to hump up in front of the bridge abutment. The water, trying to make its way through the canal, looked decidedly unhappy at finding this obstacle. I began to wonder if we would have to stay at the dock until the next slack tide. I casually asked the dock attendant about how fast the current ran.

"Oh, about two knots," came the reply.

It looked faster than that. Small twigs shot past the hull. How would we leave? Sailboats are not really good about backing up. In fact, backing up is what sailboats do the worst. I generally avoided backing *Vagus* up at all costs. The jugs were full. I asked the attendant for assistance.

"Don't worry, Skip!" the dock attendant shouted. "I do this all the time." This was said with all the confidence of youth. I figured the fellow had maybe seen about seventeen summers.

I started the engine. The attendant and I pulled *Vagus* as far upstream on the fuel dock as she could go. Now we had a little over two boat lengths in front of the abutment. I had visions of the current grabbing *Vagus* when we released the dock lines and hurtling her into the abutment. Karen was having the same concerns. With all the confidence I could muster, I suggested a plan.

"Stay aboard, Karen, and take the lines from the dock attendant. The attendant will throw you the bow line first, then he will release the stern line."

As the attendant undid the bow line, I threw the engine into reverse and tried to hold *Vagus* against the current. The attendant then untied the stern line and I turned the wheel to starboard. The action of the current against the rudder pushed the stern in and the bow out. I then put the engine in forward, gave her lots of throttle, and turned the wheel to port. *Vagus* shot out into the canal - widely missing the abutment, just like I had imagined. Amazing.

"Well done, Skip!" shouted the attendant as I casually coiled the stern line while motoring away. It was always important to look cool when performing any docking maneuver. Karen came back to the cockpit after putting away the bow lines.

"That went well," she said. "How did you know that maneuver?"

"I read about it," I replied. "It seemed like a good time to try it. Although I was a bit worried about the distance to the abutment." I had been more than a bit worried. It was actually way up there on my worry scale. I had no idea how it would work in practice. It was just one of those things that one planned out, improvised, and then did. Karen was impressed.

*Freighter in C&D Canal*

After this fueling episode, we were on our way. We headed out of the C&D Canal and up the Sassafras River to Georgetown where we had agreed to meet J.P. and Colette. From there, we again planned to part ways as we wanted to sail to Baltimore to see the big city lights. The trip up the Sassafras was all we imagined the Chesapeake to be. It had twists and turns, little anchorages off to the side, tree-lined shores, and rolling hills. We slowly motored along, drinking in the experience. Near Georgetown, we found *Safina* anchored in a side creek by the marinas and anchored behind them.

After settling in, we went by dinghy over to *Safina* for Happy Hour. There was a hurricane named Isabel in the Atlantic. For several days, we had all been tracking the storm. J.P. planned to download the latest weather information from his HAM radio system, something I still had to get working, and we were going to discuss our plans. The outlook did not look good. Isabel was classed as a Category 5 hurricane, the highest category possible, indicating the worst possible storm. And it looked like there was a chance it would head up Chesapeake Bay, right where we were! The storm could reach our area in about four days. We discussed the options. J.P. and Colette decided to stay at Georgetown to ride out the storm.    We had already booked into a marina in the inner harbour of Baltimore.  We decided to go there and, if we did not like it, would then head up a small creek nearby, hoping to find a place to hide out from the storm.  We would leave for Baltimore in the morning.

Early the next day, we got up to overcast skies.  We raised anchor, said our good byes to J.P. and Colette, promising to get together again in Annapolis at the boat show, and headed out the Sassafras River and into Chesapeake Bay.    Cruising Chesapeake Bay was a whole new experience.  First, Chesapeake Bay is shallow. Most of the Bay seems to be less than fifteen feet deep with good portions about ten feet deep. There are narrow channels for deep-water freighters but, outside the channels, the water is decidedly shallow and murky.  We could not see more than a few feet into it so there was no hope of reading the water depth.  We just had to rely on the depth sounder to tell us when the water was too thin and take comfort from the fact that most of the bay had a soft mud bottom.  And there are crab pots!  With every crab pot there is a float.  On exiting the Sassafras River, we looked out onto a sea of crab pot floats.  There was nowhere to turn.  Crabbers only put crab pots in waters less than twenty feet deep.  Of course, this applies to virtually all of Chesapeake Bay except the shipping channels.  As each pot costs about $50, we did not want to run over one.  Of even more concern to us, of course, was the danger of fouling our propeller.

After a short while, we started to see patterns to the floats.  Crabbers would run a series of crab pots out in a row, then run another row back parallel to the first.  The pots within a row were fairly evenly spaced. We could pick our way between rows by watching the float spacing and jogging between lanes.  Karen stood by the companionway with the binoculars and pointed at crab pot lanes.  I tried to steer a slightly drunken path towards our destination, missing the floats.  It was total concentration as the floats on some of the pots did not float all that well. There were so many pots we wondered how any crabs survive in the Bay.  After a short while, we turned back to the shipping channel.  It was easier to travel in the shipping channel, dodging the big ships and barges and taking a longer route, than to fight our way through the crab pot lanes.

It was just as well we did. Shortly after we reached the channel, the sky darkened and it started to rain. Karen quickly hopped down the companionway stairs and, protected by the dodger, looked out at me getting soaked at the wheel. Actually, Karen was down the stairs before the first raindrop spattered on the deck. Over the years, she had developed a finely tuned sense of impending rain, and, not seeing why we both should get wet, normally retreated below at the first hint of moisture. The skies opened. It was a Noah's-ark-flood type rain. The raindrops bounced off the water. The visibility went to 5 feet. I turned on the radar and moved to what I thought was the edge of the shipping channel. I looked for marker buoys or crab pot floats; either would show the channel edge. Through the rain, I saw the ghost of a sailboat. The boat was anchored in the crab pot field, waiting out the storm. As we still had quite a distance to go to Baltimore, we kept plodding along. Karen passed out my foul weather jacket and a dry shirt.

The rain still came. As I glanced back, our inflatable dinghy wallowed behind us. Something was wrong. I slowed the boat, then slowly pulled the dinghy alongside *Vagus*. It was half full of water and filling fast from all the rain. The dinghy would have to be emptied before we went much farther as the dinghy tow rings could not take the load without breaking.

I called to Karen, "Take the wheel. I have to empty the dinghy."

Karen looked at me and, giving me a clear-eyed stare, stated, "You are not going out in the dinghy and leaving me all alone aboard in the middle of a shipping channel! What happens if we get separated?"

"But we are off to the side of the channel," I said. "And there is nothing on the radar."

Karen, surveying the situation, made a decision. "I'll bail the dinghy. You handle the boat and don't lose me!" She went below to get into her bathing suit and foul weather jacket.

The rain started to ease as Karen climbed into the dinghy with a small bucket and pump. I let the dinghy fall back and motored slowly to keep *Vagus* at the channel edge. Karen, soon drenched in the warm rainwater, sat in the dinghy, furiously scooping the water out.  I smiled as I looked forward. Now if only I had the camera.

# 10. *The 50 Year Storm*

$A$s we approached Baltimore harbour, the sun finally broke through
the clouds. We motored towards the inner harbour in brilliant sunshine,
discarding foul weather clothes as we went. After several twists and
turns, the waterway ended in a small circular bay, right in the heart of
Baltimore. Baltimore has done much to revitalize its downtown core and
ringing the bay are aquariums, museums, stores and restaurants. I had
always wanted to visit the city by boat and now we were here. We found
Inner Harbour East Marina neatly tucked in a corner of the bay. The
marina was well protected from all sides, was very new, and had floating
docks that rode on pylons. These pylons extended well above the street
level.

"The city will flood before docks float off those pylons," I thought.
We liked what we saw, called in and headed for our slip.

The slips had fingers along either side of the boat - pure luxury. We
had a choice on which side to get off! I left Karen to clear up the boat
and walked up to the office to register. I also wanted to check on the
marina's policy if the hurricane headed our way. I had heard some
marinas make docked boats leave in the event of a hurricane and I did
not want any surprises. I asked to see the marina manager and was
greeted by a very busy, but friendly, man. Although he had just closed
the marina to any more visitors, *Vagus* had been allowed in as we
already had a reservation. The manager was trying to minimize the
loading on the docks in case the storm arrived. Further, he stated, if the
storm came our way, *Vagus* could stay, but we couldn't. He did not want
anyone aboard during the storm. The staff would be too busy looking

after the marina to worry about people as well. Karen and I had already talked about our plans if we got caught in a hurricane and had agreed that, after preparing *Vagus* for the worst, we would seek shelter ashore. Boats were easier to fix than people. This condition, therefore, was no problem and I signed *Vagus* into the marina. Marina patrons were being offered a reduced rate at the Marriott Hotel just a few blocks from the marina. I called the number given and reserved a room, just in case.

*Tied up in Baltimore*

The next day the weather report was not encouraging. Isabel was still on track to make landfall near the mouth of Chesapeake Bay and to come straight up the bay. Present estimates put it at Baltimore in two days. Baltimore had not been hit by a hurricane in 50 years. It was one of those statistics that we had looked at in choosing a location - so much for statistics. Baltimore was due for a hurricane and we were there. After giving the marina another inspection, we decided we were as protected there as anywhere. An advantage to staying in Baltimore was we were able to get shore accommodations, something we were not sure was possible if we anchored somewhere up a creek.

We began to prepare the boat for a storm. I pulled out my notebook where I had carefully made a preparation list. *Vagus* was soon spider webbed to the docks with double lines and chafe protection. The sails and canvas were taken down and stored away. The deflated dinghy was also stored below. The inside of the boat filled up rapidly. It was a long day. We collapsed that evening.

The next day the sun was out. It was a beautiful summer day. The winds were light with only a few clouds in the sky. You would never believe that, 30 hours away, a massive storm of great destructive power was approaching. There was no advance warning except for all the forecasters giving hourly updates on Isabel's progress. Never having experienced preparing for a hurricane, I wandered the docks and talked to other boaters who were getting ready for the storm. I looked at their preparation techniques. When I saw something I had not thought of, I quickly jotted it down. I hit a gold mine when I came across a catamaran on the end dock. The owner was from Florida and had been through a few storms before. He was busy duct taping all the openings around his lockers and his ports.

"With the wind," he said, "the rain will get into any unsealed opening. This is how we do it in Florida."

That sounded good to me. I hurried back to *Vagus* to impart all this newfound wisdom to Karen. Karen was a bit overwhelmed by this point as she had been getting everything secured below in case the boat was bounced around. She had thought I was working on deck, not doing one of my walk-abouts. I had a habit of wandering off at the strangest times. She would happily think I was doing a particular job, go looking for me, and find me off talking to another boater about something entirely different. I was teaching her patience. My saving grace was I usually came back with good ideas or information that we could use. I am not shy about asking questions. Sometimes she would get upset with me, asking why I asked a particular question when I had previously told her the answer.

"Just trying to get another viewpoint," I would counter.

So I came back all excited. There was more preparation to do! Carefully, we taped around all the hatch openings. We agreed that in the morning, before we left the boat, we would tape around the companionway boards in case the rain came from astern. Karen also had the idea of draping the navigation table and book shelves in a plastic tarp in case water found its way in. *Vagus* had always been a dry boat, but this was a hurricane. Karen finally took a break and went to the marina office to get the form for the discount rate at the Marriott Hotel.

The office attendant said, "Oh, you are from *Vagus*! My husband has been following what you are doing and copying you. He thinks you have the best prepared boat in the marina."

Karen thanked her and picked up the form. "Jim does have his good points, even if he does take forever," she thought. By this time, we had had enough for the day and went to explore Baltimore.

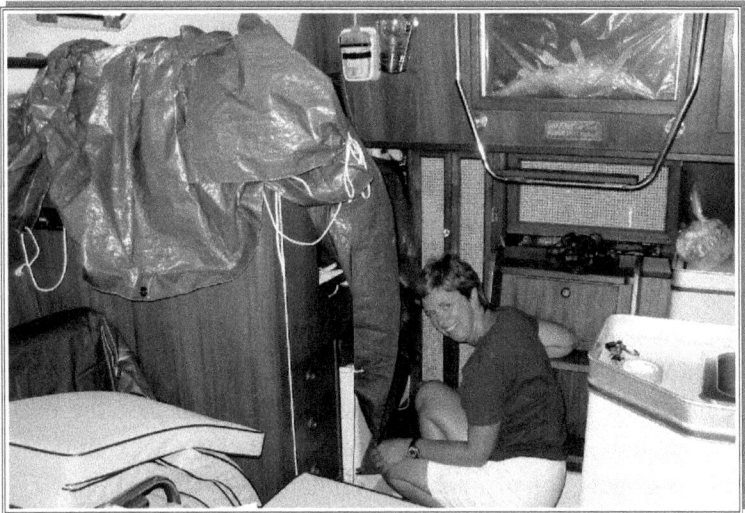

*"Plasticizing" Vagus*

The next morning the weather report was grim. Isabel was on its way. It would likely be downgraded to a tropical storm by the time it reached Baltimore, but a tropical storm was bad enough. As well, heavy rains accompanied by an 8-foot storm surge was predicted. We finished the last minute taping jobs and packed our overnight bags. Stepping off *Vagus,* we looked back at her, nestled between two large powerboats, with every line we owned connecting her to the docks. We had done everything we could. We just hoped it would be enough and she would be there when we came back. With one last look, we headed to the hotel. The rain had just started.

The hotel was beautiful and we enjoyed the luxury of an en suite bathroom complete with shower and plenty of hot water. The room also had television, something not seen since our Ontario days, and an Internet hookup. We were able to connect our laptop, surf the web and catch up on all our e-mails.

"Guess what we are doing?" we began in letters to our friends.

Our room was on the 7th floor and, from the window, we could look down on the marina. We could even see *Vagus* floating at her dock. The sky got darker and the rain came down harder. Wind gusts hit the building, rattling the windows. *Vagus* looked to be doing alright. She bounced around a bit, but nothing like she had experienced at her home marina in a storm. The television showed the destruction as Isabel churned its way up the Chesapeake. The heavy rains and storm surge seemed to be doing a lot of damage. We thought of J.P and Colette in Georgetown and hoped they would be safe.

Through the night, we took turns going to the window to check on *Vagus*. She continued to do well, but the docks were rising on the pylons. Listening to our hand held VHF radio, gusts over 60 knots were reported by people aboard boats in other marinas in the area. Still *Vagus* hung on. Finally the lights went out and we could see no more. We retired to bed.

At first light we arose and looked out the window. The street by the hotel was flooded. Water was almost to the hotel front entrance. The flood surge had gone over the banks, flooding the historic Fell's Point area of Baltimore. The docks seemed to be holding but I wanted to check on *Vagus*. We quickly dressed and walked to the marina. The rain had stopped. The docks were within two feet of the top of the pylons! The exhausted marina crew, now relaxing with a cup of coffee, had been up all night checking on the boats and the docks. Water now lapped near the marina office doors. Everything held but the crew was worried about the docks riding over the pylons during the high tide around noon. It was not clear whether the storm surge had stopped. It would be close.

*Baltimore underwater*

We returned to the hotel to grab some breakfast and check out. When we got there, the hotel was without power. Water had flooded the basement and the hotel had been forced to shut down the generator. It was good news for us as we were given free breakfast. The cash registers wouldn't work without electricity and the hotel couldn't keep the food hot. It was also bad news as the elevators and lights were out and our baggage was still on the seventh floor. The hotel staff guided us up the seven flights of stairs, dropping chemical light sticks like breadcrumbs to guide our way. We reached the airless room, packed our bags in the dark, and hiked back down the stairs. The hotel was busy trying to find room for their guests in other hotels in the city. We instead headed back to *Vagus*. We now had more facilities on our boat than most of Baltimore.

We climbed aboard. *Vagus* looked fine, as if nothing had happened.

She was dry below and everything was where it was supposed to be. I made a mark with tape on the pylon to monitor the rise of the marina. I checked on the half-hour, making a new mark. The water level was dropping slowly. We could breath again. We had survived the 50-year storm. As we started putting *Vagus* back together, we thought, "It's good to be home!"

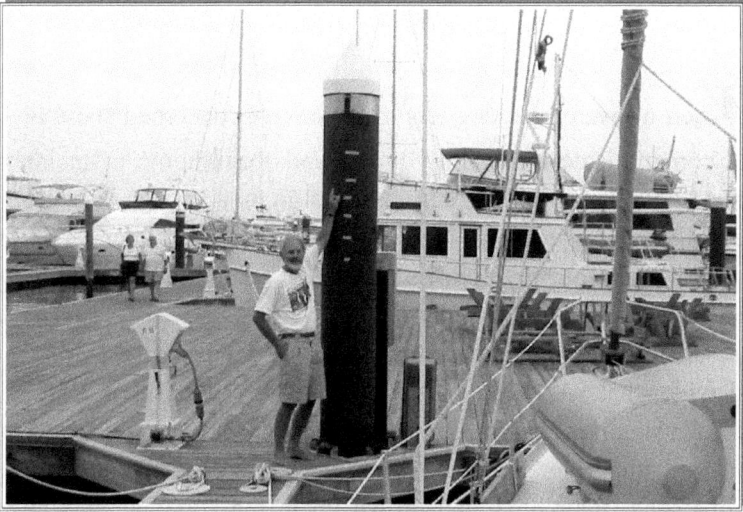

*Watching the water recede*

# 11. HAM

*W*hen we were planning this trip, we were concerned about how we would communicate with family and friends back home. Our intention was not to disappear into the sunset but to go on a voyage of exploration while still keeping in touch with our roots. Besides, keeping in touch also meant we could get updates on all the cold weather and snow we were leaving behind! After a bit of research, we decided to get our Ham licenses. Ham volunteers had recently created a series of land stations, world wide, that we could connect to and download or upload e-mail messages using our Ham radio. The ability to keep in touch, at least by e-mail, was important, as this was our normal means of communication with our sons. Our boys had grown up in the computer age and had never quite figured out the mysterious workings of the telephone, at least when it came to phoning the parents. They did monitor e-mail. So whether we were one hundred meters away or a thousand kilometers away, our boys would not notice the difference as long as we could e-mail. As well, weather information and weather charts were available through Ham. Getting a Ham license was made easier when a club member, who was also a Ham instructor, offered to put on a class for club members.

Great," we thought. Although it was a few years before we were to leave, getting our license at this time would give us plenty of time to get set up.

The Ham course started in October, right after the boats were lifted from the water for winter storage, and ran for eight Saturday mornings. We could complete our Basic level before Christmas and then take the

Intermediate level after Christmas. The Basic course was fun. We trotted off every Saturday morning for a pleasant time with club members, drinking coffee and learning new things. We felt like we were getting closer to the trip. We were doing something. We were preparing. I could almost feel the salt water on my face as parts of Ham radios were discussed. Besides, we got to talk about a whole set of new electronic goodies that I knew nothing about. Out came the notebook. On a new page I wrote "Ham Equipment". I also found out the name of THE store to go to for Ham stuff. It was in north Toronto and I convinced Karen to go for the drive. It was a whole new toy store. I was familiar with the insides of Marine chandlers by this time, but this was entirely different. I had no clue what a lot of the items were for. It was a brave new world! I now had more questions for the instructors.

To get the Basic license, we had to receive a mark over 80% on a written Ham test. The date for the exam approached. Two weeks before the exam, I pulled out my notes and books.

"I guess we'd better start studying for the exam," I suggested to Karen.

"Yes," she agreed, "but why are you looking in those books?"

Now Karen had enjoyed the Ham classes. That is, she enjoyed the social aspects of the classes, the interesting stories the instructors told, getting together with other sailors, and talking about our plans for next season. As soon as the instructors started to "talk technical", Karen would get a glazed, far away look in her eyes as her mind gently wafted over a warm sea and a sandy beach. I knew that look. I often got it from Karen when I started to "talk technical". When the boys came for dinner and started to get into the finer points of computers, they also got that look. Karen has the belief that if it is important she will figure it out when she needs to. And she felt she did not need to know the inner workings of a ham transceiver to pick up and speak into a microphone.

So Karen looked at me with all the books out and said, "I can't read that stuff. It puts me to sleep."

"But this stuff may be on the test," I exclaimed.

"There has to be a better way," replied Karen as she headed towards the computer.

Karen had always done well in school. I could never figure out why. I would study and cram for an exam while Karen would make sure she got a good night's sleep. I waited to see what she would come up with. A little while later, she came back with a mound of paper. Karen had listened when the instructor had told us how to find the web site that had every question that had ever been asked on the exam, and the answers to those questions. There were, after all, a finite number of questions that were possible. She laid out her plan. We would study the questions and answers to one section a night, and then test each other. Karen also quickly came up with acronyms for remembering the components that make up different pieces of ham equipment.

"Just remember the acronyms and write them down on the exam paper as soon as you start." I listened. I was in awe. I knew I was in the presence of a master exam writer. She knew what she was doing.

"This might work," I thought, and it was a heck of a lot easier than my method.

We studied the sections and tested each other until the day of the exam. Quietly, we drove to the clubhouse. I was trying to keep the different acronyms straight in my head. If I was unsure of one, I would test Karen who rattled it off like it was second nature. I knew she did not have a clue what the various parts actually did but she knew how they all went together. Well, if the truth were known, I also was not really sure what the different parts did either. I had an idea, though, and thought I could find the section in the book. But that was all.

People excitedly gathered for the exam. There is something about exams. I could feel the nervous energy as I entered the building. Some people babbled, some were quiet, some got there early, and some waited outside and came in the door at the last minute reading their notes along the way. I was busy repeating those acronyms in my head. Finally we took our seats and the exam started. I immediately wrote down the acronyms.

"Great," I thought. "Now I can forget those and focus on the exam."

I recognized many of the questions and, with building confidence, plowed on. The exam time was two hours. After a little over an hour, the first person got up and went down stairs to the common room where the examiner was going to mark the exam. Shortly after that, Karen got up and left. I felt a bit of panic in my throat. I still had another page of questions to go. I calmed himself. She usually finished early, I told myself, remembering years ago when we took the VHF radio exam together. She was a quick exam-doer, I thought, and got back to the test. I could hear voices from the room below as people gathered after writing the exam. I put my head down and slogged on. Finally I finished - fifteen minutes ahead of the deadline. I picked up my papers and headed downstairs. There was quite a group there by now, drinking coffee and talking excitely about the exam. I handed my answers to the examiner, who placed them on the top of the pile, and went to the coffeepot. Karen asked how I did.

"Alright, I think," I said pouring some coffee. "The acronyms that you made up really helped. It gave us several easy marks."

Karen smiled.

A little later the examiner had finished marking the tests and he called everyone together so he could read out the results.

"Not out loud," I thought. "The whole club will know how I did."

The first result he read out was Karen's. She got the highest mark, tied with another club member, of 98%. He kept on reading out results. Finally he got to my paper.

"92%," he called. I could breath. I had passed, but did not beat Karen.

"Oh well," I thought. "It wasn't a race and she does know how to write an exam!"

We now had achieved the Basic level, but still needed the Intermediate level Ham license to communicate on the high frequency bands. These bands were important for long distance communication and using the e-mail system. The Intermediate level required that we be able to send and receive Morse code at a rate of five words per minute. It sounded straightforward. We bought a Morse code key. I, a little wiser, waited for Karen to come up with a study plan.

"There's no use in even thinking about how to learn Morse Code," I thought. Sure enough, after a few false starts, Karen found an Internet program that helped us hear and send Morse code at different rates. We decided to learn at ten words a minute, hoping that would make it easier to pass at five words per minute on the exam. For the next few weeks, I thought in Morse code. I translated all the road signs into dots and dashes as I drove to work. I spent hours each night on the computer sending and receiving until I thought I was ready.

On a Saturday morning in late February, when everything was the coldest and bleakest, we went to the clubhouse for the exam. First we did the sending part. I had always found sending easier and, with a slightly shaky hand, managed to get the words off so the instructor gave me the nod. Then it was the receiving. This was the tough part. The instructor had a computer that gave a Morse code sentence at 5 words per minute. I was nervous. The instructor cautioned us that if we did not get a letter to carry on to the next letter. We started. Halfway through, I got stuck on a letter. I heard more sounds and knew I should carry on, but my brain refused to let go of the untranslated letter. By this time, several more letters had been thrown out of the computer. I was lost. I put down my pencil and looked around. Most of the class was looking around while the computer continued its discourse of dots and dashes. At least, I was not alone. At the end, the instructor asked if anyone got the message. No one answered.

"Well," he said, "let's call that one a practice run" and he set up the computer for another go. This time I got a little further along before losing it. Karen almost got the whole message. Only one person in the class, in fact, passed. She was a musician. They say musicians are good at picking up Morse code. That left me out.

Next Saturday, after another week of thinking in dots and dashes, we were back. The pencil felt slippery in my hands but I was ready. We were off. I made it through the whole message this time. I just made too many mistakes, but at least it was an improvement. Karen passed. She was finished. I had to go on.

Another week at it - by now I had memorized all the road signs as dots and dashes and could "dit and dah" them miles before actually seeing the signs. I worked the computer program every night. I did not want to continue this any longer. As well, the instructor said that this was the last Saturday he was available for a few months. If I did not pass now, I would have to live until the spring with the Morse test hanging over my head. Karen stayed home. I sat once more in the clubhouse, poised. I cleared my mind, took several deep breaths and waited for the start. I wrote furiously. The letters formed into words. When the instructor asked who wanted to be marked, I put up my hand. The instructor came by to check my finished sentence. I passed! I let out a sigh of relief. I, too, was finished. Life was good.

At least, I thought I was finished the hardest part. What could be difficult about installing a ham system on a boat? It turned out to be no easy task. I had to learn about ground planes, RF grounding, soldering connections and, of course, crawling around and reaching into difficult-to-reach spots in the boat. Shortly before we left our home marina, the ham system was installed. We could listen to different stations but we could not send effectively. And the e-mail program in the computer was not talking to the modem, an item that connects the computer to the ham transceiver. It just was not working and it was time to leave on our trip. I wrote "get e-mail going" on the To-Do list and we left.

We were now in Baltimore and, as I scanned the To Do list, "get e-mail working" glared at me. I had realized after talking to J.P. that I had bought the wrong modem. I needed a much newer, much more expensive model that promised higher speed connections and a simpler setup. It even came with special cables that connected directly to our brand of transceiver. Before the hurricane, I had ordered the modem. It would be here in a week. Everyday I checked with the marina office until it came. I am always amazed that something so small can cost so much. This unit, however, had the latest upgrades so we could connect to the high speed shore stations - still slower than a low speed land connection, but definitely better than what we had. I installed the new modem and software, turned everything on and .... it worked. Or it gave every appearance of working. It had all connected together, just as promised. It had been easy. Something must be wrong. I tried to tune in a station. There *was* something wrong. The antenna tuner was not tuning. The new program indicated when the antenna tuner was on the correct frequency for transmission and nothing was happening. As well, the tuner was supposed to make little clicking noises when it was tuning and there was no clicking. I then realized that the tuner had not clicked since I had installed it. I read all the troubleshooting manuals. One item to check was the wiring between the transceiver and the tuner.

"It's all new!" I thought, but realized I had to inspect it again anyway. This check involved taking apart the electrical panel and most of the navigation station to get at the wiring runs. And, of course, I had to remove everything from the quarter berth to get to the antenna tuner, which also had to be disassembled to check the wiring. I knew how hard it was going to be. I had, after all, installed it. It was one of the reasons we had reached Baltimore before I tackled this job. Karen, sensing the magnitude of this project, had wisely disappeared. I pulled out the shielded cable and my trusty multimeter. I tested the cable - it had a short. After all this time, I had found the problem! I replaced the cable, turned on the transceiver and tuned a station. The tuner made nice comforting, clicking noises, a light came on the transceiver saying that it was tuned and all was right with the world. That evening, we sent out our first e-mail by ham. Everything worked and it had only taken four months.

# *12. Birthdays*

*I* awoke early. We were aboard *Vagus* at the marina in Baltimore and Isabel had passed. Today was my birthday – fifty-five! I got up and put the kettle on the stove to make coffee. Karen was still asleep. I enjoy the quiet of the morning; a time when people are getting ready to go and do something. My job today was to have my birthday. Fifty-five only comes around once. I thought back to my 40th birthday. For some reason I remembered that one. I remember rolling over in bed on the morning of my 40th birthday and telling Karen that there were no professional baseball players in the Majors over forty years of age. I remember feeling a sense of loss, of missed opportunities. Karen mumbled a reply that she did not know that I wanted to be a professional baseball player. I didn't. It was just that now... I couldn't. Karen went back to sleep.

With a hot cup of coffee, I went to the navigation table and picked up my day-book. Each day's events were written in the day-book to keep a record of our trip. Neatly taped on the page for today's date was a piece of paper with a poem. I smiled. It was a poem for my birthday. Years ago we had given up buying cards or presents for our birthdays. Instead we would write the other a short poem and leave it somewhere for the birthday person to find. Karen had remembered, and put it where I normally looked in the morning. I felt warm. It had the words "fifty-five" interwoven in the lines.

"I'm really fifty-five," I thought.

I did not feel fifty-five. In fact, I felt I had stopped aging after the sudden realization of turning forty. Fifty-five is one of those landmark ages. An age when one is supposed to do something. I guessed that I was doing something. I had just retired and taken off into the sunset. That should count for doing something but I had never really tied those events to my age.

I took my coffee out into the cockpit. The morning sun streamed in. A skipjack, a picturesque, working sailboat built for harvesting oysters in the shallow waters of the Chesapeake Bay, sailed by. All the sails were flying as the boat plied the muddy waters on the bay. The bay was still very muddy and full of branches, trees and all manner of flotsam from the storm. The marina manager had told us it would take at least a week for the Bay to clear and did not recommend moving until then. There was still lots to see and do in Baltimore so we had decided to stay and explore. I sipped my coffee. I loved the aroma and warmth in the morning. It was my favourite time. This turning fifty-five, though, somehow bothered me. I was on the one hand happy and thankful to be fifty-five as the alternative was definitely less attractive. But I had a vague unsettled feeling, as if something should be different. It really felt like any other day and in many ways it was. But it was the first birthday that I would not be home, at least at a home where family was nearby. I would not get the birthday telephone calls or have an off-key rendition of Happy Birthday sung to me. I missed that. I realized that I missed being surrounded by those closest to me as I started on a new year.

Karen was up. She came over to the companionway, and asked what I was doing.

"Just thinking," I replied, and thanked her for the poem.

"What were you thinking about?" asked Karen.

"Just stuff," knowing that Karen would to try to get me into a "what are you feeling" type of conversation if I was not careful. To be honest, I was not sure what I was feeling. Well, except I was hungry, as it was time for breakfast.

"That's good," said Karen. "I was worried you wanted to play baseball again."

Over breakfast, we decided to take the day off from all the boat jobs and see Baltimore. The city was getting back together after the hurricane and most of the entertainment centers were open. It would be a day of fun and exploration. We wandered through the aquarium learning about many of the fish and mammals that we hoped to come across on our travels. When it was time for lunch, we found the James Joyce Tavern. Seated at a booth by the window, surrounded by books and old English tavern memorabilia, and looking out on the people walking by in the warm sunshine, we enjoyed a pub lunch with draft Guinness. We talked. We enjoy talking together normally, but today we agreed to avoid talking about boat jobs or travel plans. Today was our day off.

After lunch, we toured the USS Constellation, a beautifully restored sailing vessel built around 1870. We saw cannon firing demonstrations, musket loading time trials and cutlass fencing displays, and explored the interior of the ship. The construction was incredible. We lost ourselves in a time long ago. We realized we were traveling in luxury compared to what sailors on these square-riggers had to endure. After the tour, hand in hand, we walked back to *Vagus*, still talking. I prepared our "grog" Happy Hour drink, a mixture of rum, water and a twist of lime, and we sat in the cockpit, toasting the day. Karen went below to prepare dinner. I stayed in the cockpit, looking out at the boats, the buildings, the sky and, in reality, nothing at all. I was grinning, not just smiling; grinning. There is a difference. Tomorrow, we would have to start getting ready to move. We needed groceries and fuel and several boat jobs still had to be done. But today was for enjoying and enjoy we did.

What a great way to turn 55!

# 13. Up the Creek

*T*wo weeks on the dock of busy Baltimore had been an interesting experience. But now we were ready to explore the creeks of Chesapeake Bay. The first creek we picked from our cruising book was Ridout Creek. It was one of the many small creeks between Baltimore and Annapolis and had a good write-up in the guidebook. After carefully plotting out our course, we dropped the dock lines and motored out of the marina. We were now ready, at least mentally, for all the crab pots and were prepared to play dodge ball with the floats. To get to Ridout Creek, we first had to reach Whitehall Bay, follow markers around a large shoal in the center of the bay and head up Whitehall Creek. About a mile up Whitehall Creek, we had to hang a left into Ridout Creek and pick a spot to anchor. All looked good and we had a sunny day for the trip. We still had to dodge logs and trees that were around the entrance to Baltimore but soon we were slowly steaming up Ridout Creek with its tree-lined banks. Houses were nestled amongst the huge trees and docks were stationed like sentries along the shore for their owners. That was one of the problems with most of the creeks. There was nowhere to get off the boat as all the land along the creek was private. It was still a beautiful creek - our first official Chesapeake Bay creek. The creek went on in the distance. The charts, however, showed the water depth to be below 5 feet beyond the next turn. I was motoring up to the turn when Karen, with a slightly concerned tremor in her voice, asked, "Where are you going?"

"Just checking out the anchorage," I replied. "They say you should scout out an anchorage before deciding where to drop the hook." I thought I sounded quite nautical.

"Does this scouting include running aground?" queried Karen, the concern level rising a notch as the worry gene kicked in.

We came nearer the turn in the creek.. I recognized the signs.

"Okay, why don't we drop the anchor off to the side of the creek, just in front of the turn. That way we will be out of the way of boat traffic."

We were still relatively new to the art of anchoring or the "anchoring dance". Eileen Quinn, a Canadian songwriter and cruiser, has a song out by that title. She captures the whole anchoring experience well in the song. We did not know that when people anchored in these creeks, they just motored up and dropped their hook in the middle of the creek and let other boats go around them. With vagaries of currents and tides, it was just easier to be as far from each bank as possible. I thought we had to anchor off to the side to let others pass. I motored to the turn, the water depth dropping as rapidly as Karen's eyebrows were rising.

At the last minute, I spun the boat around and said, "This looks like a good place."

We were in seven feet of very murky water. We had no idea in which direction the bottom shoaled. Karen took the wheel and I went forward to release the anchor. She was making muttering noises that I knew I should ignore. Pretending not to hear, I hurried forward.

When anchoring, one partner normally handles the boat as the other goes forward to manage the anchor. The combination of the motor running and the distance apart makes verbal communication almost impossible. Impossible unless one shouts as loudly as possible to make oneself heard. Of course, by doing this, everyone else in the anchorage can clearly hear what is being said. When a shouting match happens, other cruisers in the anchorage drop what they are doing, come out to their cockpits, and watch another "anchoring dance" in progress. It is usually great entertainment. As we did not want to get on this particular entertainment circuit, we had devised a series of hand signals to communicate. When an appropriate signal was not in our repertoire or someone was uncomfortable, we would give the conference call sign. This meant I would go back to the cockpit and discuss our options or concerns. I had just dropped the anchor and Karen was giving me the conference sign, with feeling. I headed back.

"I'm not happy," she stated. "As I was backing up, the depth was still dropping and we are too close to that bank."

"Other than that, it looks like a good spot," I said smiling, trying to lighten the mood. It was entirely, and, in every fashion, the wrong thing to say.

Karen gave me the "seven letter word for a donkey's rear end" look and words tumbled from her mouth.

"The creek is too small. I don't know how anyone anchors here. I want to go to a dock. I should not have come. I want to go home!"

I now had the picture. I knew Karen did not mean all those words – well, maybe the ones about it getting shallow. It was just her way of expressing concern. It was the same as when men yell or swear at each other during a sailboat race for not doing something fast enough. It was not personal. Calmly, I said that we would raise the anchor. I had spotted a good, deep section just up the creek and we should try there before moving on. Gently, trying to calm her by my body movements, I walked toward the bow. We lifted the anchor, moved to the deeper spot - which I noted was where Karen had wanted to stop in the first place before I insisted on exploring up the creek (I would not mention that) - and dropped the hook. It held and Karen put the engine in reverse to set the anchor. She turned off the engine. The sound of birds and crickets filled the air. She quickly spotted a heron looking down from a tree. I came back.

"This looks like a great spot," she said as she gazed around.

It was a great spot. We could sit in our cockpit, which was like the back porch on a house, and enjoy an ever-changing view as *Vagus* swung at anchor. We spotted jays and kingfishers. The heron also made frequent flybys. We got out the barbeque and enjoyed dinner and the sunset. The next day, we took the dinghy and explored up the creek, running aground in the process. We had managed to avoid running aground in *Vagus* but we grounded, and grounded well, in the dinghy. Fortunately it was soft mud and we plowed our way out. The water depth was impossible to read due to the muddy water. And there really were lots of shallow areas.

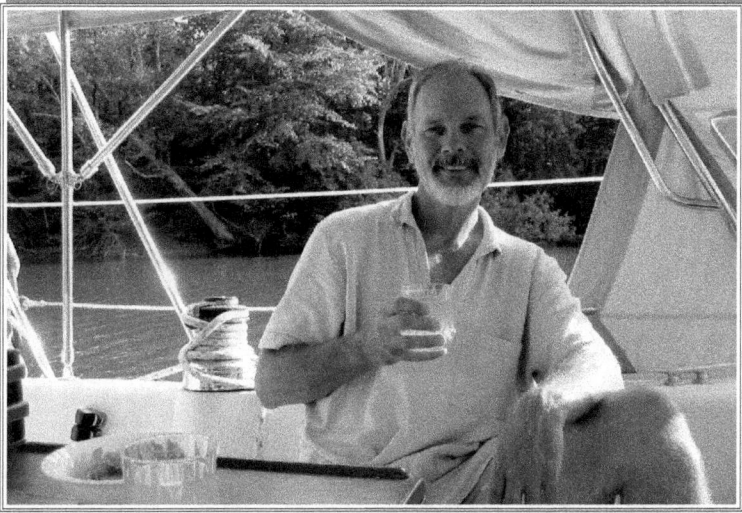

*Enjoying our "back porch"*

Although we enjoyed the privacy of a beautiful anchorage, we began to feel a lack of exercise after a few days as there was no place to land and walk. Karen decided she wanted to take the dinghy out for a row. This was an event I looked forward to and I got out the camera. Karen is a good rower but an inflatable dinghy is notoriously hard to row. People normally avoid rowing an inflatable at all costs. The answer, if one wants to row, is to buy a hard dinghy. Karen climbed aboard with her life jacket, emergency dinghy kit, dinghy anchor and line, hand-held VHF and bailing bucket. It took about half an hour but she was prepared. I cast her off, checked my watch and took my first picture. I gave her 10 minutes before she would get tired of rowing. The dinghy drifted off in the current as Karen got the oars from under the seat and installed them in the special holders. These holders had looked like excellent oarlocks when we saw the dinghy at the boat show but, as the oars could too easily slip overboard, they were awkward to set up and use. Finally she got the oars in place and positioned herself on the fiberglass seat. She was now about thirty feet from *Vagus*, gently moving with the current. She started rowing, moving up the creek and over to explore the shoreline. I took another picture. She was rowing quite well. I thought that it did look like fun. I put away the camera, picked up my book and settled in for a good read in the cockpit. Karen stayed out well past the 10-minute mark I had given her. She was exploring. Going where she wanted to go. Going where she had never been before. She was smiling. She was having fun.

*Karen gets exercise*

# 14.  The Boat Show

## *Arrival*

*A*nnapolis is a boater's town.  It is definitely all about boats.  The creeks around Annapolis are lined with boat yards, marinas, and more boats than we have ever seen in one place.  The creeks are literally a sea of masts.  Every year in mid-October, Annapolis hosts a sailboat show - some would say "The Sailboat Show".  It has become a major drawing card for sailors everywhere.  The show date is at a time when the majority of sailboats are making their annual trek from the north to warmer climates and Annapolis is right on the route.  It is a recipe for success and a "must stop" for cruisers heading south.  All the major boat builders are there, showing off sailboats that we normally only see in magazines.  The suppliers of all the bits and pieces that, again, we had only read about, are also there, presenting a candy store of "must haves" and "want to haves" for a sailor's pleasure.  There are also non-stop seminars offering advice on whatever there is to learn about sailboats and cruising.  It is an event to look forward to.

We pulled into Annapolis about a week before the event, hoping to find an anchorage near the show.  We were lucky and picked up a mooring in Spa Creek on the other side of the bridge from where the show was going to be held.  As stated in the guidebook, we radioed the marina office and gave them the mooring number.  The office replied that a launch would be sent out to collect the fee.  The launch never came. The next morning, as honest cruisers, we went to the office to check in.

"Where are you?" the manager asked. "We've been looking for you." Apparently we were at the wrong mooring. We had picked up a private mooring by mistake. Luckily there was another mooring available nearer the bridge as the anchorage was quickly filling up. We moved *Vagus* to the new spot and settled in.

The first order of business was to find J.P. and Colette, who had anchored in another creek (Back Creek) near Annapolis. Contacting them by VHF, we were invited aboard *Safina* for Happy Hour. Getting there was easier said than done. The trip to *Safina* involved motoring the dinghy to a street access on the shore. Annapolis has set up dinghy tie-off areas at the end of many streets to allow cruisers to get ashore – a good business proposition as one can't spend money unless one can get ashore. It was then about a kilometer walk to get to another street dinghy access on Back Creek. From there, we called J.P. on the hand-held VHF. He then picked us up in his dinghy for the trip to *Safina*. It was worth the trek as we renewed our friendship and told "Isabel" stories. J.P. and Colette had survived without any damage but had spent quite an anxious night. It was great seeing them again and we planned some outings together, one of which was to get some warmer clothes.

## The Shopping Trip

*T*he days had become colder and the nights were downright nippy. We had already pulled out our little alcohol heater from the quarter berth to take the edge off the fall evenings. We now needed thermal underwear. The next day, we met with J.P., and Colette for the "great clothes shopping trip". Deciding that our best bet was a large shopping mall on the outskirts of town, we worked out a route to get to the mall on the public bus. The mall turned out to be a large one, with lots of stores. Thinking it would be more efficient to split up, we agreed to meet later for lunch.  The mall wandering began.  Shortly after parting ways, we both ended up at the one outdoor store in the mall that had a good supply of all those lightweight, high-tech, ultra-warm, and expensive clothes. Carefully, we chose hopefully warm things.  It was tiring work.  We were not used to malls or to shopping.  J.P., before he left on their trip, had stocked their boat with clothes in the belief and hope that he would not have to go shopping again.  He didn't just hate shopping; he could not stand it.  Now he was trapped.

Karen and Colette had bonded and were off trying on various things and discussing the various items' relative merits.  I was in the store's camping section trying to figure out how a flashlight, that was supposed to work without batteries, actually worked.   I had learned to amuse myself during shopping trips.  Shopping trips with Karen, by their nature, took a long time.  I had long ago come to peace with this fact and normally got into a Zen of looking at items that I did not need but looked interesting.  I noticed J.P. standing, looking straight ahead.  He did not look happy.  J.P. looked at his watch, then back into space.  Karen and Colette had secured the changing rooms and were going through the "getting the right size and how does it look" phase.  I could not resist.  I caught J.P.'s eye and moved into the role of "help the girls by being the runner".  I knew this role.  Whatever Karen first chose would not fit so she would need the same thing in a different size.  Soon, I was moving about the store, picking up items for both Colette and Karen.  Other customers started asking me for help.  J.P. now had his arms crossed.

On the next trip, as I passed by J.P., I asked, "Do you think Colette would like this little Polartec vest that I picked out?  It's only $80."  I kept going quickly, a small smile forming as J.P.'s face turned red.

I laid the acquisitions out for the girls, turned around and grinned at J.P.  J.P. rolled his eyes and started to laugh.

I came back, grabbed J.P.'s arm and steered him out the store saying "I told the girls we would meet them at the restaurant bar.  Let's go for a beer."

As we departed, J.P. was still mumbling how he hated shopping, but he was smiling.

# *Mooring Life*

*L*ife on a sailboat at a mooring presents its challenges. Four necessities of life are showers, laundry, drinking water and "what to do when the holding tank gets full". These are fundamental issues that we have to learn to deal with when we stop in one spot for awhile. The holding tank turned out to be the simplest problem to solve. Chesapeake Bay is a no-discharge zone so the tank contents could not be pumped overboard. "What to do when the tank got full" was solved by the local pump-out boat, a service run by a local marina. When we needed a pump-out, all we had to do was call the marina and book a time. The pump-out boat would come alongside and relieve *Vagus* of stuff we prefer not to think about. The operator was a semi-retired Captain who was a delight to talk to. He still did charter runs and usually had a story of some adventure to pass the time away while business was being done. I looked forward to our chats.

Showers and laundry were a little more difficult. The shower and laundry facilities are at the marina office. A shower involved getting all showering equipment, including towels, together. Yes, I have in the past forgotten my towel. I found, from experience, a face cloth worked quite well for drying – as long as I noticed my towel was missing before using the face cloth for the shower. From the mooring where *Vagus* was located, the marina office was a fifteen-minute dinghy trip under a bridge and up a stretch of water in front of the downtown core. This piece of water is referred to as "Ego Alley" as new owners of fancy and expensive yachts would parade their new acquisitions up the alley for all to see. The marina dinghy dock is at the end of Ego Alley. Arriving at the dinghy dock, we would first lock the dinghy from curious bystanders - this was the downtown, after all. Shower tokens were obtained from the marina office. Then it was up two flights of stairs to the showers. If we were lucky, the showers would be available.

The laundry machines are also in with the showers. There are machines in both the men's and the ladies' shower areas. It was not uncommon for the ladies' machines to be full as, apparently, more ladies do laundry than men. Resourceful ladies, when finding their machines busy, would use the machines in the men's.

"Close your eyes," they would say. "I'm coming in to get my laundry," as I stood on one leg trying to dry my foot after a shower. Ladies can be jokers. Showers were a bit of an event and had to be planned with the detail of a military campaign. With showers done, we would return to our boat to hang the towels to dry, a tricky task if it happened to be raining. Some days it was not worth the effort. On those days, we tried to stay aboard, or at least well bundled up.

Drinking water was another story.

"Where can I get fresh drinking water?" I asked the marina manager on the first day of registering. This was a very important question as it was not intuitively obvious.

"It's on the post at the end of the square," he replied.

I looked for the post. The marina office is on Ego Alley. And Ego Alley dead-ended at a small square where there are a number of seats and a plaque commemorating Kunte Kinte's arrival on a slave ship. The square is surrounded by small shops and is a nice place for tourists to gather and view the harbour. Directly in front of this square is the dinghy tie-up dock, and, off to the right along the breakwater, is a post. On the side of this post is a water tap with a sign. Neatly written on the sign is "Potable Water".

"Ah, that must be the tap!" I thought.

We could get water. *Vagus* holds eighty gallons of fresh water, divided into two tanks. When one tank ran dry, it was the signal to do something, such as get more water. Karen was particularly good at getting me to keep track of the water level.

"Lots," was my normal reply when Karen asked about the water remaining. Karen knew not to let go.

"How much is lots?" she would ask in a certain tone. After over thirty years of marriage, I knew that I had better pay attention when she used that tone.

"Maybe I better check," said I. It was a daily ritual. We each knew our parts. Our lines were well rehearsed. We would not feel right, as if a line were missed; if the water ritual was not followed.

The day came when we needed water. A battle plan was needed. We had one water jug that held five gallons and two jugs that held two gallons each. We wanted to take on close to thirty gallons. It was a real life arithmetic lesson. We figured it would take four dinghy runs to the water tap. Karen had not been present when I researched the location of a water supply so, before leaving to fetch water, she thought she had better make sure we weren't going on a blind quest.

"Do you know where the water is?"

"No problem, the water is at the dinghy dock," I replied.

One of the interesting facts about cruising full time is - it is easy to lose track of the days. Every day feels pretty much like the one before. The "gotta go to work Mondays" had become a thing of the past. Unknowingly, we had picked a Saturday to get water, a beautiful Saturday afternoon. A time when many people with have better day recognition skills sauntered down to the lovely downtown core to go shopping and eat ice cream cones. As we motored down Ego Alley, we looked at all the people. There were people everywhere. Ahead of us the dinghy dock waited, full of dinghies. Dinghies were three deep out from the dock. Dragging full jugs over all those dinghies at the dock was not an option. This was going to be difficult.

I came up with an idea. I would drop Karen off at the dinghy dock then motor over to the wall that had the water tap. Although the wall was six feet off the water, Karen could fill the jugs and pass them down to me as I held the dinghy in place below. Karen was not amused but could not think of a better idea. It was definitely not her idea of fun. She scrambled over the dinghies as people eating ice cream cones started to take notice. People have a sixth sense when they feel something interesting is going to happen. This looked like it was going to qualify as an interesting event. Karen reached the post and politely asked several spectators to move away so she could get water. This, of course, initiated a series of questions as to why she was getting water, what she did with it, and what life was like on a sailboat. I passed her a jug and she started filling. She felt very "Third World", as if she was going down to the village stream for water. It was hot. The water splashed. The jugs were heavy as she held them under the tap. More people came, stared, and asked questions. During this time, my mind turned to ice cream.

"A cone would be nice on the return trip," I thought. "Karen," I said, without really observing how she was doing or her present frame of mind. "Why don't you pick up a couple of cones after you are done?" I turned to look at Karen in the ensuing silence.

Her eyes were giving me the seven-letter word glare. Excusing herself from onlookers, who at that moment were giving her advice on how to minimize splashing, she replied, in a very controlled voice, "I don't think that would be a good idea, dear." We only made one water run that day.

## New Friends

Another Canadian-flagged sailboat sat on a mooring near us. The boat had come in while we were in town. We had seen this boat before at Chesapeake City. It had come into the anchorage in a major downpour and, at the time, we had felt sorry for the couple as they anchored the boat in the wind and rain. It was a traditionally designed, wood sailboat, about thirty feet in length. Everything was wood, including the mast, and she looked fairly new. She also looked like a sturdy, go-anywhere type of boat that some of the cruising legends would have sailed around the world with no motor and only kerosene lanterns. She was quite pretty in a functional sort of way, dressed up with tan bark sails. There was no dodger or bimini, just a small cockpit with tiller steering. The owners were exposed to the elements. We, in contrast, had a full enclosure around our cockpit.

We decided to visit. It was common to go over to other Canadian boats to say "hello" and exchange histories and plans. We pulled alongside the boat in our dinghy and rapped on the hull, calling "Ahoy!" Two heads quickly popped out of the companionway. With quick introductions, we were invited aboard.

"All we have is rum," said Ed. "Would you like a drop?"

"Rum sounds great," I said as we sat down in the cockpit. Their names were Ed and Robin and they were from New Brunswick. Ed was an unemployed shipwright. He needed something to do so Robin suggested that he build a boat. We were now sitting on that boat. The boat was entirely built by Ed, everything from shaping the masts to casting the lead keel. It took him about three years - fast considering all the work that was required. I was impressed. We were invited to see below. It had one cabin; one cabin that they shared with a new two cylinder Yanmar diesel engine, the major purchase for the trip. On either side was a bunk for sleeping and sitting. Ed poured a measure of rum in two glasses and handed them out. He poured similar measures in two mugs for them. They only had two of everything. Their water tank was a 5-gallon plastic jug. But their boat below was warm and cozy. It felt comfortable. Ed gave the full tour, telling how he made the different items. The wood had all been locally grown. He also talked about the next boat he would build, a little bigger with a few more amenities. This boat had been built for this particular trip. They planned to be gone for a year as Robin had only a one-year leave from her work. From Annapolis, they would head south to Florida, then cross to Cuba. They had always wanted to visit Cuba and had made arrangements to see their daughters, who would fly to Cuba in February. After visiting Cuba, they would head north to return home.

The new diesel had been installed at the last moment when they realized, with all the motoring on the ICW, they needed a good engine. We talked on, changing topics like the wind. Ed poured more rum and soon we noticed it was dark - time to head back to *Vagus*. We invited Ed and Robin over for happy hour the next day and said our good byes. We would see Ed and Robin throughout our time in Annapolis. It was great sharing ideas, plans and dreams with other cruisers - people who had come from different backgrounds, who had different types of boats, who had come from different parts of the country, but who all had similar dreams and had acted on those dreams. Ed and Robin included us in their group e-mail list that gave up-dates on their travels. They made it to Cuba in time to see their daughters. Last we heard, Ed and Robin were nearly back home.

## *Exploring*

*W*e started to fall in love with Annapolis. The core area of the town was easy to walk around. It was actually the best way to get around. We had been there long enough that we started to get a sense of place. We could confidently direct other cruisers, new to the area, on how best to get to the local stores. We took a sightseeing tour and learned about the history. After, as we walked around, we could point to the various landmarks, remembering the guide's rather laconic description of events. The guide had interjected a dry sense of humour into his presentation that had made the tour entertaining. As well, we spent a day touring the Annapolis Military Academy with J.P. and Colette and watched 4200 midshipmen march in formation to the mess hall for the noon meal. In general, we were starting to get a feel for Annapolis and the people who lived there.

We were settling in. In the mornings, we would dinghy to the town docks for our showers. After breakfast, we would head off exploring. Everyday we would walk through a different part of town, remembering the tour's history lessons: Annapolis, originated in 1649, was named after Princess Ann, Queen Mary's daughter. It was once the capitol of the U.S. The Treaty of Paris, ending the revolutionary war, was ratified in the state house situated in the downtown core. The state house occupies one hill and St. Anne's Episcopalian Church occupies the other, slightly lower hill, symbolizing the separation of church and state. The roads leading up these hills are lined with an array of beautifully restored Victorian and Georgian buildings. Many of the streets are quite narrow and the buildings colourfully painted. Apparently the restoration society regulates any external changes to these buildings with the exception of the building colour. The occupants make full use of this singular freedom of expression.

It was the first time that we had experienced such a sense of place while traveling. "This is an unexpected bonus of cruising," we thought. "The ability to stay and enjoy a particular location." It was another lesson in the gentle art of cruising.

## *Old Friends*

*I*t was time for the boat show. We had been watching workers assemble the dock systems that would hold all the boats for display. Wood pylons had been driven into the harbour bottom around Ego Alley and docks materialized like magic to fill the bay area. The dinghy dock had been moved to a side street by the Naval Academy. It was a much smaller area and was now normally very crowded with dinghies. I would plow into the dinghies while Karen would hang over the bow trying, like Moses, to make an opening. Usually we had to settle for scampering across the other dinghies with a very long tie-up line when we made our morning shower run. The showers were also starting to get busy with all the show personnel that delivered the show boats. If we wanted a shower, we had to get there early.

We were excited, though, because our friends from Ontario, Daryl, Ann, Bob, and Sue, were driving down and were due to arrive the next day. They would be staying in a motel but we had arranged to meet at *Vagus*. Our friends had been given a description of the street where the dinghy dock was and Bob would call on his portable VHF radio when they arrived. Fortunately it was sunny when we got the call. Our friends were here! It was reunion time. First the group toured the St. Michaels area by car, an area we had not seen, enjoying crab cakes, a Chesapeake specialty, for lunch. Returning to *Vagus*, we took a dinghy tour of the anchorage and enjoyed Happy Hour aboard *Vagus*. Karen had snacks ready and we were soon making plans for the next day. We would go to the boat show but also fit in a short walking tour of downtown Annapolis, with us as tour guides, of course.

The next day the sun was again out, the flags were flying and it was time for the show. We wandered the docks, visited boats that none of us could afford, and looked at the incredible boating toys available. We were thrilled to hear Eileen Quinn at one of the seminars. Eileen is from Ottawa, cruises full time, and writes and sings about her adventures. We are big fans. It was a fun day, a day without formal structure, a day just to enjoy. After a short walk along some of the more colourful streets, imparting our newfound knowledge, we found a small pub just outside the show grounds and managed to get a table by the window. With pints all around, we toasted friendship and the day. The waiter offered to take our picture. It was a good shot, one that we saved. It became a one of our favourite pictures. One that we cherish. It was a cool day, that day of the show, but whenever we look at this picture, we feel warm.

# 15.  *Cruising the Bay*

*T*he boat show ended and the temperature fell.  Mornings were very brisk - very, very brisk.  It was time to head South.  We had planned a leisurely trip down the Bay to Norfolk but the weather was not cooperating.  We decided to keep moving until we got back to shirtsleeve weather.   The first day out, we found a deserted little cove in the Solomons.  Deserted in the sense that there were no other boats anchored there.   Houses and docks lined the cove.   But *Vagus* was alone, well tucked in from the channel.  We had wanted to find a good spot as a cold front from Canada was due the next day.  Canada was in full production of cold fronts.

"More Canadian arctic air is due," the weather forecaster said.  If it was cold, it was always from Canada.  So we found this little cove that could hold no more than two or three boats and anchored in the middle, trying not to block anyone from leaving their dock.  We settled in.  It was a quiet night.

The next day, we took the dinghy to town to pick up some supplies.  Along the way we saw Ed and Robin motor by on *WaveWalker* and head up another branch of the creek.  We tried to wave but Ed and Robin were intent on making it to wherever they were going to anchor.  According to the guidebook, the only place we could land a dinghy was at the Holiday Inn dock near the end of one of the inlets.   There apparently was a grocery store nearby.  Although we first missed the inlet, we finally saw, after a few twists and turns, what we thought was the Holiday Inn.  Spotting another couple in a dinghy motoring purposefully towards what appeared to be a dinghy dock, we went in hot pursuit.  On arrival, there was even an attendant.  I thought that this was a nice gesture from the Holiday Inn until the attendant asked us for two dollars to tie up for an hour and another dollar for our bag of garbage.

"Everything costs money," I thought.  We had not seen another spot of land anywhere along the way where we could have stopped for free. We paid the money and headed to the store.  Laden with fresh groceries, beer and water, we returned to *Vagus*.

The weather was starting to deteriorate as we zipped the full enclosure around the cockpit.  The plastic panels would allow us to enjoy the outside without getting cold or wet - hopefully.  The forecast called for another severe front to come through that evening.  The wind had already picked up and a boat that had anchored at the entrance to our cove rocked in the waves as the wind blew down the channel.

"Maybe it won't be too bad," I thought..  After an early dinner, we prepared for bed.  One thing that we had learned was if bad weather was coming, it would arrive late at night.  I never figured out how the weather managed this.  There is something about gently nodding off for the night that sends a signal to the weather saying "It's time!"

About 11:00pm, the front came through.  It was like a wall of wind. The wind speed suddenly increased and swirled; the rain came down in sheets.  It was as if a fire hose was being sprayed back and forth across *Vagus*.  I put on my foul weather jacket and headed for the cockpit for the anchor watch.  The drumming of the rain against the plastic side curtains made talking impossible.  I checked our position.  We looked alright except the wind had changed direction.   All the familiar landmarks that I had figured out earlier in the day were now at a different location.  A house in the cove had a light on and I used that as a new marker.  As *Vagus* rolled with the gusts, the light stayed in position.  We were holding.  The GPS was already on so I checked our position.  Our position had changed as *Vagus* swung with the wind, but now it was steady.

"At least we don't have to contend with waves," I thought.

Karen went back to bed, ready to come and help if there was a problem.  I settled into the cockpit seat, knowing I wouldn't be able to sleep. Trying to curl up in a dry spot, I watched the wind speed hit 30 knots. I listened to the rain pounding on the plastic. I looked for the house light. I went into a Zen of watchfulness. The engine was ready to start at a moment's notice.

About 2:00am, I noticed that the wind speed was starting to drop. The gusts were not as forceful; the rain not as hard. The people in the house had put out their light at about 1:00am, giving me a little heart flutter when, all of a sudden, the light disappeared. At least, it kept me awake! But *Vagus* was still holding and all looked well. I went to bed. We were developing what we call our "at anchor" sleep pattern. We became attuned to the ambient noise of the wind in the rigging and the boat creaking. Any noise that sounded different, a new pattern, would cause one of us to get up to check. It was the same skill developed in parenthood. Quite naturally, and without any previous discussion, each of us would get up at random times of the night to check if all was well. So I went to bed and tried to get used to this new pattern of noises. I would think of it as "front noise". Later, I checked my watch. An hour had gone by and I got up to look around. We were still holding and there was now a steady rain. I went back to bed.

"I can catch up on my sleep tomorrow," I thought.

After resting up the next day, we were off again. We had a rough sail down to Sandy Point, situated on the Grand Wicomico River. The weather forecaster got the wind direction correct. He just had a slight miss on the wind speed. It was a hard, eight hour, close-hauled sail in rough water. *Vagus* seemed to enjoy it but we found it hard having to hold onto something for eight hours. Mother Nature provided encouragement by sending us a pelican - our first pelican of the trip. We must be getting further south - nearer warmer weather! We stared at the pelican as it swooped gracefully by, our dreams riding along with it. We wondered how something so graceful in the air could look so awkward hitting the water when diving for fish. A point to philosophize about someday when we weren't enduring such an uncomfortable ride!

The next day, we had a leisurely motor sail to Deltaville. The forecast low winds had arrived.  Just a day late.  Deltaville had a challenging entrance even before Hurricane Isabel had shifted all the entrance markers.  I stopped about a mile offshore as we tried to figure out the passage into the harbour.  Luckily, we spotted a powerboat coming out.  We watched its path and could make out an apparent route.  At least, we could see the first set of markers and the general approach angle.

I called to Karen.  "We're going in!"

Karen grabbed the binoculars to look for the markers and point at their location.  The guidebook was lying on the cockpit seat, turned to the Deltaville page.  The main instruction in the guidebook, highlighted in bold print, was "not to trust its (the guidebook's) directions".  "Read the water," it stated.  "The sandy bottom often shifts due to storms." Isabel had shifted a lot of things.  The water was clearing up at this end of the Chesapeake so we could make out a change in water colour indicating different depths.  The sun was directly overhead, which helped enormously.  I headed *Vagus* directly for a sandy beach towards the point where the powerboat had made its turn to open water.  Just as I thought we were about to run onto the beach, a deep water channel along the shore on our port side opened up - just like the guide book said it should.  The channel was a deep blue colour, edged by pale blue indicating shallower water.  The deep blue part looked to be only thirty feet wide.  On we went, following the channel along the shore.  I felt I could have grabbed a handful of sand if I leaned over.  Karen was busy pointing at buoys.

"There's the entrance!" she shouted, her body vibrating in excitement.

I liked the vibrating part but I had to keep my focus.  The entrance opened up on our starboard side and we had to make another sharp turn.  We were in!  It was a lovely large anchorage.  The shoreline had taken damage from Isabel, however, and the marina was still closed for repair.  We found a spot and anchored.  Another front was due that night.

After the front, the weather report called for light winds of 10 knots and sun.  Not great for sailing, but it sounded like a good traveling day.  A long day should get us to Norfolk, about a 50 mile trip.  We raised anchor at first light, something of a challenge for us, as neither of us are morning people. As we headed out of Deltaville, we noticed other boats ahead and behind us. Boats were filing out of the many anchorages in the area. Everyone had heard the same weather forecast and all decided to move. I counted 40 masts on the horizon at one point. It was like a bird migration. I wondered where all the boats had come from. This must be the great wave leaving the boat show. We raised the mainsail and motored along. Soon the winds started to pick up, the motor was shut off, the foresail was let out and we became a sailboat. It felt great to be charging along with sails full on a sunny day. Sunny was the only part of the forecast that the weather office got right. We should have known. It sounded too good to be true, and it was. Weather forecasters everywhere have one thing in common – they are usually wrong. The wind started to build. We put a reef in the mainsail. The wind increased some more and started to shift direction. Another sailing rule is that any shift in wind direction will be in the direction that impedes progress. The wind was starting to come in the direction that we wanted to go. It would definitely impede our progress. The wind increased more and we put a second reef in the mainsail. Soon it was blowing 20 to 25 knots, with gusts to 30. We were sailing into the wind, and had to tack to make progress towards Norfolk. *Vagus* was heeled over. She was heeled over so far her toe rail was in the water and water was streaming along the deck. I pointed this out to Karen.

"I've never seen *Vagus* heeled over so far!" Karen grunted and was concentrating on finding a more comfortable spot where she could sit and hold on at the same time. I found hand steering quite exhilarating for the first hour.

The waves continued to build. Chesapeake Bay is relatively shallow and waves tend to have a very short, uncomfortable pitch. *Vagus* was now slicing into one meter waves that continuously threw themselves at her. I tried to pick a smoother path through the waves. I missed one set and *Vagus* fell off a two meter wave. An eight ton boat falling two meters makes quite a bone-jarring splash. The kerosene lantern, hanging in the main cabin, came down at a different time than the rest of the boat. Karen went below on a search and rescue mission. Amazingly, nothing was broken. There was just a big dent in it that would inspire this story.

I started to see *Vagus'* bow burying in the waves. Massive amounts of water were coming over the bow and running in rivers down the side decks. As I watched, I remembered that I had not sealed the hole where the chain drops through the deck into the locker – a locker that drained into the bilge. I had presumed it was going to be a light air day so had not bothered. At about this same time Karen, having rescued the lamp, returned.

Sounding frightened, she said, "There is water up to the floorboards." My heart sank. Water from the anchor locker had filled the bilge.

"I forgot to seal the anchor locker," I confessed.

Confession may be good for the soul but, at that point in time, what Karen was thinking was not good.

"We better heave-to and seal it," she said. "There is a lot of the Chesapeake down there."

We stopped the boat by heaving-to. It was amazing. The books said that the boat motion eased when one hove-to and they were correct. We had never hove-to under such rough conditions before. We went from a state of being thrown around to an almost comfortable, cork-like, bobbling motion. I tethered myself to the jack line and crawled forward on my hands and knees to the anchor locker. For penance I was splashed by the occasional wave that roared by. After sealing the chain hole, I went below to pump the bilge dry. I waited to make sure that it stayed dry, changed clothes and grabbed some cookies. Karen maintained look out. Soon we were underway again. I was hand steering. *Vagus* was doing really well and we were making good speed considering the conditions. The conditions were just unpleasant and uncomfortable. We checked if there were any anchorages closer by. We were in the middle of the bay by that point and any anchorages were far up channels, about as far as it was to carry onto Norfolk. An alternate destination was chosen – we would go to an anchorage by Hampton at the entrance to the Bay. Hampton was fifteen miles closer than Norfolk, a significant distance at sailboat speed.

It was a long day. *Vagus* did well. We did well. The winds eased late in the afternoon and, finally, we found ourselves approaching the shipping lanes at the entrance to Chesapeake Bay. The anchorage at

Hampton opened up to the starboard. There was lots of room and we headed in. The elation of having made a safe harbour after a tough day overcame our exhaustion. We had reefed the boat, we had bailed the boat, we had hove-to, and we had sailed – oh, how we had sailed! One of the longest sails of our trip so far. Certainly the most difficult. And we had made it to our destination. As we were tidying the deck, we spotted another Canadian boat. The skipper was waving to us and motioning us to monitor the VHF radio. We were invited over for a cup of tea after we finished dinner. We agreed on a time. We gave each other a hug and smiled as we started dinner. We could cleanup tomorrow.

# The Waterway

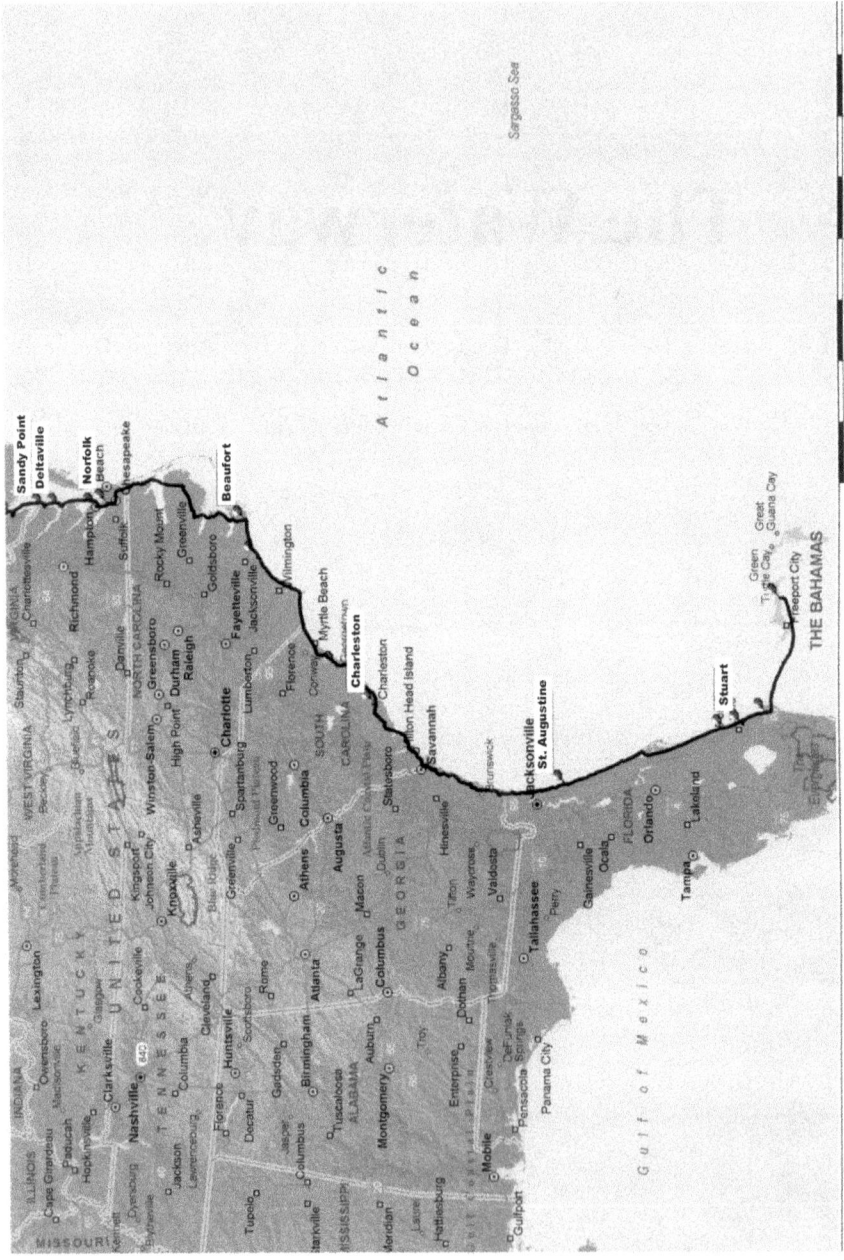

Intracoastal Waterway from Norfolk, Virginia, to Florida

# 16.  Big Ships

*A*fter our rambunctious sail down Chesapeake Bay, everything was salty.  We were salty.  *Vagus* was salty.  The crystals on the deck had the effrontery to glisten in the fading light of the sunset; they did not enhance the sunset.  Little salt crystals assailed our feet, dropping off as we moved about down below.  The bilges were salty right up to the floorboards, and our bedding was salty.

Earl and Martha had invited us over for tea after we arrived at the Hampton anchorage.  After a delightful evening, they said, just as we were getting ready to leave, "We are going to take a dock at Waterside Marina in Norfolk tomorrow to cleanup and wash the boat before heading out on the ICW."  They normally did this.  Earl and Martha had done the ICW in the past and their words had the weight of experience.  Also, what they said made sense.  A cleanup was definitely at the top of our agenda.

We looked at each other, and in one of those moments in a married couple's lives when mental telepathy seemed to be at work, we turned and said in unison: "We will meet you at the marina sometime tomorrow."

We left *Pleasure* for a salty *Vagus*.

*Pleasure* raised anchor early while I was making breakfast.  Breakfast is normally my meal.  Well, not normally - it is always my meal.  I like breakfast.  Breakfast is not just my meal; it is my favourite meal.  It is what starts my day.  I could not imagine a day without breakfast.  It isn't so much what I have for breakfast, although I do like a variety of things, it is just, well, I really like breakfast.

So after a really good breakfast, we raised anchor and left for Norfolk. We called the marina while underway to ensure a dock was available. We were now looking forward to a good clean up. To get to the marina, we had to motor past the naval shipyards. Coming from Canada where one rarely saw a naval ship, mainly because naval ships are quite rare, we were amazed by the collection of naval ships of every imaginable size and description. And these were the ones at dock. There was a whole row of aircraft carriers. Canada does not have an aircraft carrier. There were submarines. There were destroyers. And there were odd-looking ships with big doors and lots of antennas. I called these "support ships" when Karen asked. I did not really know but thought that anything without an obvious big gun on it must be a support ship of some description. I decided that being a naval architect for the Navy must be an interesting job.

"They get to design all these neat, strange-looking vessels, specially designed for some exotic purpose. It must be like being let loose in a Lego factory and told to build something." Several ships were in dry dock and had been raised above the water level. It was amazing to see a full size ship sitting proudly on the shore. Some had their underwater areas shrouded to keep away prying eyes. What exotic underwater shape or propulsion system was hidden there? We could not get too close to the vessels as, lurking in the shadows beside the ships, were high-speed powerboats containing people in uniforms holding big guns. They did not look friendly. There was a mega-buck fine if a private boat got too close to a naval vessel and those people looked like they would not be shy about enforcing the rules. When the channel narrowed, markers around the vessels indicated the proscribed distance to keep away. And there were tugs. Tugs of different sizes were scurrying around the channel, getting ready to move something or coming back from securing a ship in her berth. All in all, it was an interesting trip.

Soon we were at the marina. *Pleasure* was already there. Earl had a hose out and was attacking the salt on his boat. *Pleasure* was made of steel and Earl had a special passion about keeping the salt off. We pulled into a slip beside *Pleasure*. It was time to start the cleanup process. Even though Karen or I could do virtually any of the jobs on *Vagus*, somehow the chores while on board fell along traditional male/female roles. I normally cleaned the outside of the boat, Karen the inside. Karen did the laundry; I maintained the engine. She did the cooking and dishes; I tried to look busy at those times. We both did the provisioning. So I joined Earl in cleaning the outside of the boat and Karen joined Martha in the Laundromat. All was right with the world. It was a big cleanup job, but the day was beautiful and the sun was warm. We had a lovely spot and could watch the tugs and big ships going up and down the channel, as well as keep an eye on the private boats as they went by.

The marina was right by the sign marking mile zero of the ICW. We had been traveling for three months and had gone over 900 miles just to get to mile zero. But it was the starting point for a new phase of our adventure. Norfolk was a good spot to orientate ourselves for this next phase. Karen and Martha came back with the laundry just as Earl and I finished the boat cleaning. I was always amazed how this worked out. Karen seemed to have a sixth sense of when I just finished a job, materializing ready for whatever came next. It was late in the day. Earl suggested that we go to the local restaurant by the marina as he saw that it had two-for-one pitchers of beer and cheap wings for Happy Hour. The suggestion brought a smile to my face.

"Cheap wings and beer, alright!" We agreed to meet after showering. The restaurant turned out to be a Hooters franchise. I remember the evening as one of those perfect ends to a great day. We sat on a balcony talking with now good friends, overlooking our boats and the channel; the sun setting, drinking beer, and eating wings that were brought in a continuous flow by a lovely young lady. "It just doesn't get any better than this," I thought.

The decision of going to a marina turned out well. A grocery store sent a van twice a week to pick up cruisers at the marina, take them to the store, and return them after shopping, for free. It was a wonderful service. We were brought back by the store manager who gave us a brief history and tour of Norfolk. As well, we were within walking distance of the Naval Museum and the USS Wisconsin. The USS Wisconsin is a huge battleship on display. We could walk the teak decks and stare up close at the 16-inch guns. The ship is immense and requires 1600 sailors to run it. That would be a provisioning bill! Later, we took a half-hour bus trip through Norfolk to the West Marine store to get a new VHF radio. Ours had been making strange sounds and several times just did not work. We wanted something reliable when going along the ICW. And Karen met her heroine in, where else, the Laundromat. She was doing a final wash before we left and had met a fellow cruiser. I was not sure how the subject came up, but this woman had said that the only things she did on their boat were the laundry and the navigation. Her husband had wanted to do this trip and she had agreed as long as they would not anchor and she would not have to cook. Her job as navigator was to ensure that they found the next marina and, from there, the restaurant. I could see that Karen was rolling these thoughts around in her mind.

"I had better nip this one quickly!" I thought. "What about all those beautiful anchorages and sunsets and candlelit dinners in the cockpit they are missing?" I suggested.

"Yes," said Karen. She sighed and, with a far away look in her eyes, wandered below to put away laundry.

# 17. Follow the Yellow Brick Road

*W*e were off - Mile Zero of the ICW!  It was early morning and cool.  No, it was cold.  Dressed in my thermal underwear, Polartec vest, foul weather jacket and pants, winter gloves and toque, I climbed behind the wheel.  Well, I more or less "waddled" behind the wheel.  I had carefully arranged several cushions so I could sit high at the helm seat and see over the dodger to follow the marks.  The ICW has special symbols on the day markers and special day markers where regular markers are not present.  Each marker has a number, making it possible to track one's position by checking off the markers on a special strip chart.  The ICW is also laid out by the mile.  Anchorages, towns, bridges and rivers are all quoted as at "mile xx" on the chart.  As we knew where we were and where we wanted to go, it was a simple matter to calculate how far to the next destination.  This chart covered the whole ICW in a booklet form.  Karen had already laid out the chart book and had clear post-it-note tabs ready to place on our position as we moved from mark to mark.  That was her job - to keep us from getting lost.  This was the start of a whole new phase.  We estimated that we would have to travel about a thousand miles along the ICW to get to a spot in Florida where we could jump off to the Bahamas.  Today, we would tick off the first miles along the road.

At the thumbs up signal, Karen cast off the lines and climbed aboard.  *Vagus* motored out the marina and towards the channel as Karen put the lines away.  We knew our respective roles.  We did not need to talk; we just went into our "getting *Vagus* underway" routine. We had developed many such routines. One of our sailing instructors had once insisted that all docking maneuvers be conducted with grace and decorum. He would have been proud of his pupils that day - no fuss, no talking, just purposeful movements. In the channel, we joined other boats heading south. In fact, there were a lot of other boats. We were in the midst of the annual migration and would be traveling almost convoy-style for most of the trip. It was a foreshadowing, but it had not registered as yet.

*Migration of the Snowbird Sailors*

We soon came to our first bridge. We were using a guidebook by "Skipper Bob" that gave a mile by mile description of events along the canal. The book stated that this bridge was a railway bridge and it was always open. The bridge was closed - we were at Mile 1. A train had decided that, on this day, it would use this bridge and play "switch cars about" by backing on and off the bridge. It was a lengthy delay but at least the channel was wide and I could get a good look at an aircraft carrier that was being built at a dock near us. More boats arrived for the convoy during our wait. Finally, the bridge opened and, one by one, the boats lined up and passed through. Like geese, the boats were now arranged in formation. Some boats were slower and dropped back.

Some were faster and moved to the front of the line. But a line it was. I thought that it was no problem following the markers; I just had to follow the boat in front of us like traffic on the freeway.

Nearing a turn, we saw a huge cloud of orange smoke ahead and to the side. Suddenly, military helicopters came thundering overhead, making a low-level pass towards the smoke. High-speed powerboats charged by, full of people looking serious in full uniform, holding big guns and wearing gas masks. The orange smoke was now wafting towards the channel; the channel where we would soon be traveling. Karen's brow was working overtime. She started into her worry routine

"What is this smoke? What should we do? Maybe we should stop and turn around? Why are they wearing masks?" she gabbled in rapid fire while I watched the smoke waft in the air currents. I was still working on a reply when Karen decided to close up the boat. She managed to find some plastic to seal the companionway. At least the inside of the boat would be safe and clear. Of course, we would still be outside - a flaw in the plan - but it kept Karen busy. The military came on the radio as several boats further up the line slowed to turn around.

"All pleasure boats, maintain course and speed. This is a maneuver," the radio crackled.

Karen had just found the tape and was trying to tape the plastic in place. We kept motoring. The smoke had mostly cleared by the time we reached the exercise area. Military powerboats now lined the channel. It looked like the exercise was over. The soldiers in the powerboats were still wearing their masks. "Wonder what chemical made all that smoke?" I thought.

At Mile 6, as *Vagus* came around a bend, a group of boats ahead of us were slowing down.

"We are getting near the second railway bridge," said Karen.

According to the guide, it was also supposed to be always open. It was not. We were starting to learn the art of waiting for a bridge. We would be experts by Florida. Sailboats like to move; they do not like to stay still in one spot. Stopping a sailboat is not like stopping a car. In a car, one can put on the brakes and the car stays where the car is told.

There are no brakes on a sailboat. On top of that, there is usually wind and current in the channels near a bridge that try to move the boat in a direction one does not want to go. Just letting the boat drift to a stop and having it stay at that location does not ever happen.

As well, the channel in front of a bridge usually narrows. I blame the accountants for this fact. I am sure that, left on their own, bridge engineers would build magnificent spans at the widest areas of the waterway. This would give them more bridge to admire and to tell their grandchildren about. When accountants enter the picture, lacking any sense of beauty outside a balance sheet, they force the engineers into looking for the narrowest spot to build a bridge to costs. So all the boats, gathered in front of a bridge, would be funneled into this constricted gap with little maneuvering room.

Another unfortunate fact is that water usually shoals around a bridge, further restricting the effective channel size. Sailboats need deep water as sailboat designers like to hang long lead appendages from sailboat bottoms in an effort to keep the sailboats upright. Add all these elements together, throw in a large number of sailboats gathering, trying to hold still, turning around, and avoiding the shallow bits while waiting for the bridge - well, you get the picture. I learned a lot about how *Vagus* handled that day. All the while, I had to look cool behind the helm. Fortunately, with all those clothes on, no one could see the panic etched on my face.

The train moved across the bridge at the speed of a retreating glacier and, finally, the bridge opened. All boats now started for an entrance that would only fit one boat at a time. Somehow the boats merged into a line and the convoy was off.

*Joining the lineup to get through the bridge*

Next on the agenda was a lock. This was the only lock on the ICW and the water only dropped by two feet.

"No problem," I thought, still fresh from our Erie Canal locking practice. *Vagus* came up to the lock. There were a lot of boats to fit into the lock. Again, we had to wait. Boats were being tied up on either side of the lock. Soon it was our turn and we headed in. We were guided to a port tie up - not our favourite side, but this should be easy. The mast was even up so we did not have that to contend with. As we headed in, the wind picked up from behind. The wind seemed to funnel up the lock and I was having trouble holding *Vagus*. When *Vagus* felt wind, she wanted to go. The lock attendant told us to throw our dock lines ashore, as the lock sides were too high to get off. He would tie a line off on a bollard to stop the boat. The wind speed increased; we were getting closer to the boat that was already tied in front of us. The lock attendant wanted the boats close together to get the maximum number in, but I suddenly realized that the attendant was using the wrong bollard to snug the line. He would not be able to stop the boat. I put *Vagus* in reverse - hard reverse. She slowed and, with that sense of slow motion that sometimes one experiences when something not nice is happening, I watched *Vagus* gently coming to a halt as *Vagus'* bow light slammed into the hard dinghy on the boat in front of us. The light exploded in a shower of plastic bits. The score was dinghy: one, light: zero. The attendant finally got the dock line secure.

"Sorry, Skip. Misjudged that one!" he yelled as he walked past to get the next boat in.

I looked for plastic bits. The people on the boat with the dinghy were very nice and passed back a piece they found inside their dinghy. I saw a large piece floating away in a mad dash from the boat. It had had enough and was leaving. The light was destroyed. There was no hope of repair or resurrection, only replacement. It was our first blood. *Vagus* had made it through 30 locks and a hurricane, and a simple two-foot lock had got her.

Leaving the lock behind us, we spotted *Pleasure* at a free dock on the opposite shore. There was an empty spot. I wheeled *Vagus* in a 180-degree turn and pulled into the dock. Earl and Martha helped with the lines. We had to talk about our first day. We had been traveling six hours, had only gone twelve miles, and had quite a lesson in frustration along the way. Earl and Martha invited us over. It was time for Happy Hour.

# 18.  *What Do You Think About?*

*I* was sitting on my perch at the helm seat.  I thought of it as a perch as it had perch-like qualities.  It was high so I could have an unobstructed view over the dodger and all the deck gear.  A good view was important. I had to watch for markers, look for any hard bits in the water (branches and logs tended to find their way into the channel), keep an eye out for other boats, and keep *Vagus* within the channel.   Current and wind constantly conspired to move her out of the channel.

Comfort was also important.  I would be sitting for long periods of time.  I had taken several boat cushions and carefully arranged them into a little mound.  It was not too stable a mound as the helm seat was arched to begin with.  My cushions sat on the top of the arch and I sat on top of the cushions.  We formed a sort of fluid tower that could move with the motion of the boat.  I thought of an article I had read on how buildings are constructed in earthquake prone areas.  The buildings are not rigidly held in place but float on a special foundation, like I was doing on my perch.   The only problem came when my mind wandered, which it was apt to do, and I would lean to the side when *Vagus* decided to lean as well.   I would then accompany the cushions in an abrupt movement down the arch to the corner of the cockpit.  I called this abrupt motion my "self-wake up" feature.  It helped me stay alert, I thought.  I told people about it.  I wondered if I should send this idea to the "Things That Work" page in a yachting magazine.  After a few days, my body became self-aware of the relative motion between boat and cushions.  It was a bit like riding a horse.  My mind could then wander off as my body became one with the boat and the cushions.

131

Once stationed on my perch, I could easily grab the wheel and survey the instrumentation, all busily giving me information on how *Vagus* was doing. If the channel was straightforward, I would lean back against the push pit rail and steer with my feet on the wheel. On sunny days it felt good to motor down the ICW, arms draped over the rail, feet keeping the wheel in position, and gaze around at the passing scenery with the wind and sun on my face.

I spent almost eight hours a day for over thirty days on this perch. We would rise before first light, something alien to both of us, but necessary, in order to arrive at a reasonable time at the next anchorage. I would make breakfast and coffee. I would make enough coffee that I had some for my special underway mug. Alex, our oldest son had given me this mug - a high-tech, stainless steel, vacuum-insulated mug with a special non-spill lid. I had used this mug to take coffee on my drive to work. Now I had this mug for the drive to Florida. So I made the coffee, put on layers of clothes, and, with a final check of our route, we would raise anchor. Once in the channel, I would take my seat at the helm perch. Somehow the day would go by, and, before I knew it, *Vagus* was on the approach to an anchorage for the night.

One afternoon, as I was on the bow setting the anchor, I wondered, "How did the day go by? One minute I was raising the anchor and the next I'm setting it. What happened in between?" I should have been bored - after all, I was hand steering *Vagus* for almost eight hours. Normally I got bored with steering after an hour. "I'll keep a list of events tomorrow," I thought. It seemed like a good idea at the time.

I kept a list, but, more importantly, I consciously tried to note what was happening and what I was doing. I saw a pattern develop. I was imposing a routine on my day. Each day we would motor off into the early morning light. Karen would do the navigation and keep track of our location on the chart. I would steer. After about half an hour, I would start drinking coffee from my special mug. I had been waiting for this coffee. I did not want to start it immediately. It would still be too hot and I liked to get settled and on the way first. But after thirty minutes, I could hear the coffee calling to me. I would look for a clear spot without passing boats, take the mug in my hand, and slowly bring it to my mouth. I could smell the fragrant coffee aroma in the brisk morning air. There was nothing like hot coffee in the great outdoors. I could feel the warmth. I would take a sip, letting the hot liquid swirl in my mouth, absorbing the flavour.

"Ah," I would declare. "Nothing like hot coffee in the morning to get you going."

Karen knew those words by heart. She heard me say those same words, about half-hour after starting out, every morning of our trip along the ICW. Soon she would just mouth the words in sync with me, not really noticing what she was doing or that I was saying the words again. It became like breathing, something that just goes on. I savoured the coffee. I would wait for a clear spot without other passing boats, gently pick up the mug from the mug holder on the binnacle, take a sip, make a sighing noise, carefully replace the mug in the holder, lean back and smile. It would take me at least another thirty minutes to finish the mug. We were a good hour into our travels for the day before the coffee ritual was completed.

After the coffee was finished, I would hand the mug to Karen who would go below and do the dishes. Now coffee has an important effect on the body. It was about another half-hour after finishing the coffee, when Karen was just finishing the dishes, that the next routine began. The coffee plus the cold air combined forces to make it necessary to perform one of those important functions of life. I would call to Karen that I had to go below.

She would call back, "Could you wait while I finish clearing up?" I would then sit there. One problem with recognizing that one had to go was that one would start to focus on the need to go. The more one focuses, the greater the need. Soon the need changes to necessity. I called to Karen.

"Coming!" replied Karen as she started to apply layers of clothes.

Once in the cockpit, I briefed her on our location and what was coming ahead. Hopefully, a bridge was far off as Karen refused "to do" bridges. I soon learned to check my need if a bridge was listed on the chart. I had to plan the break well in advance of a bridge. The power of suggestion, though, was strong. There was nothing worse than knowing that I could not go at a certain time. It definitely increased the need. Soon I would feel the need to go whenever I saw a bridge in the distance, even though I had just gone. A wait at a bridge became agony.

Karen would take the wheel. Karen was not tall enough to see over the dodger unless she stood on her toes, not a comfortable position for any length of time. She could not get the rhythm of the perch so, to steer, she stood and moved from side to side of the cockpit to see forward. She did not like steering so most of the driving fell to me. After Karen was settled, I would go below and start stripping off layers of clothing in a desperate drive for the head. I braced myself on the throne - it was important to be firmly braced. I had no idea how the boat was going to move, so I had to be well planted and secure to be able to counter any odd boat movements without creating difficulties. I also had to leave the door to the head open in case Karen saw any problems ahead. If she did, she would call below.

"I need you. You'd better get up here soon."

It was not always a relaxing way to go. When finished, I would reapply my various clothing layers and return to the wheel. We had now completed hour three of our travels.

It was time for our morning cookie. Once I was back behind the wheel, Karen would ask if I wanted a cookie. She always asked and I always said yes. I did not know what would happen if I said "no" because she was normally heading below for the cookies before I answered. It didn't matter. I always wanted a cookie. Soon it would be lunch and the whole routine was repeated again.

We also kept busy checking our progress on the chart. We would make sure of our position by reading the number on the ICW channel marker. Karen would then mark our position exactly on the chart, and know how far we had gone and how long it would take us to reach the anchorage we had picked the night before. Often the anchorage was either too far, as we were slowed by contrary currents or bridges, or too near, as we had made good time and were not ready to quit. The guidebooks would be consulted again and Karen would come up with alternatives. The alternatives would be discussed and debated until a consensus was reached. Usually we had our anchorage debate just after lunch.

We also had to keep track of other boats. The ones approaching us were not a problem. I would just swing *Vagus* into their wake and carry on. The challenge was in passing and being passed. Most of the time we were being passed. Karen, who sat sideways on the cockpit seat, would be on the lookout for boats from astern. When a powerboat came up from behind, she would call out, stating which side of *Vagus* the boat would be passing on. The etiquette is for the sailboat to slow down as the powerboat reaches its stern; the powerboat also slows to minimize its wake and slowly passes the sailboat. I could then power back to cruising speed. This procedure normally worked well. Some powerboat skippers were better at the maneuver than others, but most were courteous and at least tried. A few didn't. *Vagus* would be rolled from side to side and we would find out what was not stored properly. There were a lot of boats on the ICW and many of them were powerboats. As most of the boats were heading south, the passing routine happened many times a day. Often much time was spent watching a boat approach from far up the channel to get the "slow-down" timing right. It took a long time for the approach, as speeds were restricted.

Occasionally we got to pass another boat - always a sailboat. All sailboats have a preferred cruising speed where the diesel engine hums along merrily and very efficiently. This particular speed varies from boat to boat so, when a number of boats are in a line, there is a certain amount of jockeying for position. Passing another sailboat takes a long time. It was like a Volkswagen beetle passing a Volkswagen bus on an uphill climb. When encountering a slower sailboat, I had to wait for a wide part of the channel with no oncoming traffic. I would then pull out to make the pass. The difference in speed might be all of one knot. Slowly the boats would inch together and come alongside. We could have afternoon tea in the time it took to pass. Often pleasantries and waves were exchanged as we checked out each other's boats. A good sailboat pass could occupy the better part of thirty minutes. It was to be savoured and enjoyed. It did not happen often.

Then there were bridges. Bridges cross the ICW at regular intervals. The new bridges were sixty-five feet or taller which meant they did not affect travel unless one's mast height was close to the mark. The older bridges, and there are many older bridges, have to open before one can pass through. Some bridges only open at set times. We had to time our progress to reach a particular bridge not too early and not too late. Most bridges opened on demand when there were sufficient boats waiting to justify an opening - and there was a lull in the traffic going over the bridge. The bridges were for cars after all. Our day would revolve around the number of bridges that we had to pass through. Each bridge would typically require an extra half-hour travel time. As we got close to a bridge, Karen would call the bridge operator on the VHF radio to request an opening. We would wait, trying to hold the boat still, until the operator could open the bridge, then take our spot with the other boats to pass through.

Sometimes, if we timed it right and we got lucky, the bridge operator would say "Keep on coming, Skipper. I'll open when you get here."

This was the signal to keep up speed while the bridge operator and I tried our luck at bridge roulette, a variation of Russian roulette. I was supposed to keep up speed, not slackening a bit. If I did, the operator would call back; "I'm waiting for you, Skipper. Keep it coming." So I would continue, moving at full throttle towards the closed bridge; a structure that would definitely win in any sort of duel with *Vagus*. The bridge operator, not liking to disrupt traffic, would time the bridge opening sequence to the minute. A horn provided the first indication that the bridge had started its opening sequence. Then, very slowly, the traffic barriers would start to come down. I would note *Vagus'* speed over ground and the distance to the bridge. Once the barriers were down, the bridge span would start to open, very slowly at first, like getting out of bed first thing in the morning, then faster. By this time, I was watching the bridge looming up ahead of us, my hand on the throttle ready to throw *Vagus* into reverse. The bridge and *Vagus* were rapidly coming together. I could start to read the "year built" and "dedicated to" signs on the bridge. I was getting nervous, off my perch and standing, shifting from one foot to the other, saying "It's going to be close, it's going to be close" over and over again.

Karen just sat with her mouth agape, staring at the oncoming bridge. She trusted my judgment, she thought. Soon, we were nearly at the bridge – then, just as the bridge arms were fully raised, we passed through. There was plenty of room and, probably, at least a couple of extra minutes of time. I let out a sigh of relief. Karen called the bridge operator, "Thanks for the opening."

He called, "Have a good day, Skipper."

"That was a well timed opening," he was probably thinking as he started lowering the bridge. Nobody mentioned how close it was. We got through alright and that was all that mattered.

During other moments, I found myself just looking at the ever-changing scenery. Like a train going through the countryside, our view continually changed from rugged wilderness to massive mansions. Birds and, if lucky, dolphins also kept us company. So at the end of the day, while reflecting in the cockpit as we sat at anchor, I realized why the day went so quickly. We were really quite busy.

# 19. *Gus and the Seagull*

*T*he sun was just starting to make its appearance for the day as we left the marina at Georgetown. We motored down the channel, heading for an almost hidden entrance to the ICW. A small boat sat at anchor off to the side.

"That looks like the *Seagull*," I said.

"I think you're right," replied Karen, reaching for the binoculars. "I wonder what he is doing here?"

The boat appeared empty but it was still early and her owner was probably still asleep down below. We motored on.

"Remember when we first met Gus?" I mused. It was one of those clear memories; one I knew would be with me forever. We were approaching the town dock at Little Falls, New York, on the Erie Canal. An opening appeared just in front of a small sailboat that had seen better days. From the look of it, the boat had seen a lot of better days. As we approached the dock, out of the small boat hopped Gus to help us with our lines. Gus matched the boat. He too had seen better days. He looked sort of like a scruffy ex-biker that had just finished a long ride. He was big and had the prerequisite torn black tee shirt and jeans. He was missing a few front teeth. And he had a little dog for company. The dog's name was Dawg. Gus helped us tie up and introduced himself. It being a hot day, Karen, instinctively, moved up wind. He showed us where we could get water and wandered back to his boat. His boat's name was *Seagull*. It was apt. It was his home and amounted to all his worldly possessions except for a bunch of stuff that he was trying to flog on E-Bay. We walked past *Seagull* on our way to say hello to Greg and Melissa, whom we had met earlier along the canal. We said hello to Gus along the way. He was fixing something. We would soon realize that Gus was always fixing something. Something was always broken. He was actually good at fixing things. He would pull something apart, figure out how it worked, fix it out of spare parts scattered around his boat and put it back together. Most men are good at the "taking apart" phase. Gus could put it back together. His boat below looked like a spare part storage bin. Bits and pieces of various items were scattered throughout the cabin. There appeared to be no order. There did not appear to be any place to sit. We moved on. We asked Greg and Melissa about Gus. Greg knew Gus from much earlier up the canal.

"Great fellow," he said. "Has a heart of gold and can fix anything. He will help anyone; just don't stand too close. He has a small boat and not much water."

Karen met Gus next in Waterford, New York, at the end of the canal system. She had gone to the local Laundromat and had just finished loading her clothes into the washer when Gus walked in to check on his laundry. Gus did laundry. Karen was impressed. With the second time of meeting now occurring, we were, of course, cruising friends. Gus explained how the dryers worked and how one could get the most amount dried for the least amount of money.

"You have to put all your quarters in first so it stays on the hot cycle for longer. Don't keep adding quarters or you go through a "cool down" every time," he explained.

Now Karen was really impressed. She followed Gus' advice and has passed on this wisdom from Waterford to Trinidad. I stopped by the Laundromat on my way back from shopping. I found Karen and Gus deep in conversation. Gus was telling his story. He was heading to Florida where he hoped to get a job. He only had $400 and some stuff for sale over the Internet on E-Bay. And his dog was eating up most of his money. Dog food was expensive. Karen had a good time. Gus is one of those intelligent self-taught guys who just did not fit into any particular mold. He had his own mold.

We saw Gus again anchored outside the Castleton Yacht Club on the Hudson River, waiting for help at the mast crane. At the time, we were on our way to the Catskill Creek to get *Vagus'* mast raised at the marina in the creek. We waved to each other as we passed.

The next meeting occurred when *Vagus* was sitting on a mooring at Atlantic Highland Yacht Club in New Jersey. We were waiting for a weather window to go south. Returning to our boat one day, we spotted *Seagull* anchored near the shore. And there was Gus, rowing Dawg for a shore break. We waved and Gus started to row over. Gus had a little six-foot hard dinghy. Gus filled the dinghy. There was not much free board when Gus was aboard. It looked like a small wave could come right over the side. But the dinghy did match *Seagull*. They looked like they belonged together. Gus invited us over for a beer. He had just bought some imported Becks beer. And he had only $250 left unless he sold his stuff on E-Bay. It was becoming a familiar opening. We invited him aboard. He said he would come back after he had given Dawg shore leave and dropped him back on *Seagull*.

Later that day, Gus showed up. Dawg looked over at *Vagus*, keeping an eye on his master. Gus had met up with a Florida couple and they were traveling together to Florida. They hoped to catch the next weather window down to Cape May, the same window we were looking at. Gus was busy fixing his autopilot; he hated steering. He also needed to get enough gas aboard to feed his outboard motor. He planned to sail directly to Cape May and he would be by himself. So it ended up that *Seagull* joined the small flotilla of boats that left Atlantic Highlands on an overnight sail to the Delaware. We would keep in touch by VHF radio through the afternoon and night. Gus had no problem keeping in touch as he had boosted the power on his VHF radio to twice the legal limit, something he proudly proclaimed over the airwaves. His Florida friends suggested he might not want to broadcast that fact.

"Not worried about no officials," declared Gus. We could hear *Seagull* through the night. He was having a rough trip. The wind was on the nose and all the boats had to motor sail. The Florida boat and Gus traveled about the same speed; the others, about a knot faster, soon pulled away. Gus would check in every two hours, and sometimes just want to talk. As we approached Cape May, Gus ran low on fuel. The two boats at the back turned in to Cape May while the others continued on to Breakwater Harbour.  As we sat at Breakwater Harbour over the next three days, we could clearly hear Gus talking to his friends.  We wondered if the whole East Coast could hear Gus.  Gus kept us up to date on the latest thinking of the boats waiting in Cape May for the weather to break.  It was nice to know that other people were out there.

We all left for the trip up the Delaware together - one group from Cape May and the other from Breakwater Harbour.  The two groups converged about half way up the Delaware just as the wind started to pick up.  Gus announced his progress along the way.  Part way up, his auto helm broke.  He tried to hand steer and fix the auto helm at the same time.  He had pieces spread around his cockpit and it was getting rough.

"I can't steer worth a damn when I have my hands free, let alone when I'm tryin' to fix somethin'!" he said.  Soon, he had it fixed and his zigzag path straightened.

All the boats made it to Chesapeake City on the C&D Canal.  We agreed to meet on shore.  We finally met Bill and Sue from Florida who were traveling with Gus.  It had been a rough trip.  Everyone gathered outside a coffeehouse, sharing stories before heading for supplies.  Gus gave Dawg a much needed shore break.  The weather was again closing in.

We met again in Annapolis.  We did not actually see each other; I just heard Gus over the VHF radio and broke in.  We had a nice chat.  Gus was leaving the next day with Bill and Sue.  The weather was too cold for the Florida couple.  They had all their clothing on and were still cold.  It was time for them to make tracks south.  Gus was going as well.  I wished Gus a safe trip.

Occasionally, we would pick up a transmission from Gus as we made our way along the ICW; but it was not until Beaufort, N.C., that we would talk again.  We had just pulled into Beaufort and had gone exploring by dinghy.  We met Bill and Sue on their boat.  They were planning to leave the next day with *Seagull* and head offshore down the coast to get into warmer weather.  Gus was not aboard *Seagull* when we finally found her anchored at the end of the channel. The next morning we heard Gus, though. I called him on the VHF and wished him well. Gus was friendly and happy as ever. He now only had $150 but had some more stuff for sale on E-Bay.

That was the last we heard from Gus until we saw *Seagull* anchored by Georgetown. Later that day we heard Bill and Sue calling *Seagull* on the radio. Karen broke in.

"We passed *Seagull*. She's anchored by Georgetown."

Bill and Sue were relieved, glad to hear that he appeared to be safe. The trip offshore had been much rougher than forecast and they had been separated from *Seagull*. They had lost radio communication and did not know where Gus had gone. They now thought that he had lost his radio and had taken the Georgetown harbour entrance to take a break. Gus was still on his way to Florida. We hoped that he would finally make it.

# 20.  ICW Memories

## The Great Dowry Creek Raft-up

*I*t was a quiet evening after a good day.  We had just finished dinner and were settling in to watch the sunset.  We were on a mooring in Stuart, Florida, and, every evening at this time, conch shells were blown by veteran sailors of the Bahamas, resulting in an impromptu contest between moored boats.

"I was just thinking of our trip along the ICW," said Karen.  "What were your favourite parts?"

I pondered this question for a moment.  "One that comes readily to mind is Dowry Creek," I responded, taking a sip of Earl Grey tea, piping hot, while leaning back and adjusting a cushion for maximum comfort on the fiberglass cockpit seat.

Dowry Creek occurred early in our ICW travels.  We were only two days out of Norfolk and had been traveling with two other boats of similar size, when a cold front was predicted to go through.  Earl, on *Pleasure*, had done the trip before.  He suggested Dowry Creek as a good spot to lay up for a day while the front went past.  After checking the charts and guides, the group made for Dowry Creek.  When we arrived, the creek looked ideal.  A small marina sat at the entrance with plenty of room for the three boats to anchor close by.  Shortly after we set *Vagus'* anchor, *Pleasure* motored in, followed by Dave and Barb on Mary B.

Earl liked to drive *Pleasure* well into an anchorage.  Earl always impressed me by how far in he would motor before setting his hook. I had usually chickened out far earlier, in deeper water, after watching the depth sounder steadily drop.

"How much water do you draw?" I asked Earl.

"Six feet," said Earl.

I was amazed. *Vagus* needed five feet and I would break out in a cold sweat if the water depth went down to seven feet. That, and the fact that Karen, who was driving the boat when we were anchoring, watched the depth sounder like a hawk. She absolutely refused to go any shallower than seven feet. If I guided Karen to a depth to which she did not want to go, *Vagus* would come to an early stop and I would get the hand signal summons to come to the cockpit for a conference. Sometimes, from my lack of response, Karen would get creative with her signals.

So there *Vagus* sat, floating nicely at anchor in seven feet of water. I was sure the water depth decreased to six feet about one hundred meters further on. I watched Earl calmly motor by. Earl gave a little wave as he motored on, without slowing down, for about another two hundred meters before he turned around and dropped his anchor. I watched him the whole time, waiting for *Pleasure* to come to an abrupt stop.

"I guess that's what experience is all about," I thought.

*Pleasure* anchored so far up the channel that Dave and Barb on Mary B could anchor between *Vagus* and *Pleasure*. We were the only boats to arrive and anchor. The three boats, neatly lined up the creek, had the whole creek to themselves.

Meeting by dinghy at the marina, we discovered that it cost $4 to land the dinghy, $2 for a bag of garbage and $2 each for a shower at the marina. We skipped the shower. When all were ashore, I asked Earl about his technique for going into an anchorage.

"Well," Earl replied, "No real secret. I just watch the depth sounder and anchor in seven feet of water. At least, I think it is seven feet. I still have to calibrate my depth sounder."

"That might be a good idea," I suggested.

The next day Earl and Martha stopped by in their dinghy and asked if we had ever been on a dinghy raft up.

"No," replied Karen, "but it sounds like fun."

Earl told us the plan. Everyone would meet at *Pleasure* in their dinghies at 4:00pm with their Happy Hour drinks and an hors d'oeuvre to share. The group would then motor upstream, raft together, and drift with the current until everything was consumed or it got dark, whichever came first. It was a plan - our first dinghy raft-up.

Karen layered cream cheese, curried mango chutney, and crushed peanuts in a bowl with crackers on the side for dipping. I packed the required number of cans of beer in a small cooler - my contribution. At 4:00pm, we were off in our dinghy. Clouds formed overhead but we were out of the wind. Karen insisted on bringing the foul weather gear. One just never knew. We met Dave and Barb at *Pleasure*. Earl and Martha climbed into their dinghy and cast off. The incoming tide moved water up the creek. The three dinghies, rafted together, made a convenient triangle as they began their journey. Out came the snacks and the drinks, and, slowly, the countryside went by as the raft bobbled up the creek. It was a great time of story telling as we were all sharing a similar adventure. There were a lot of snacks and it soon became apparent that dinner was not a required item on the agenda that night. We ran out of beer just as it dusk approached - perfect timing. Martha invited everyone back to her boat for cards.

When the time came to break up the raft, I had an idea. Here we were; three dinghies rafted in a circle.

"What would happen if we kept tied together, started our motors and drove in the same direction? How big a whirlpool could we make?" I suggested excitedly. The other men immediately took to the idea, their eyes lighting up. The women all started to display little worry frowns. But it was too late. Earl had started his engine and soon three engines were driving the dinghies in a rough circular motion. It was a wild ride. We did not make a big whirlpool, just several little ones, but everyone was laughing when we broke up. It was a success, of sorts, and it had just started to drizzle. The front had arrived.

"What a great day! And now we have done our first dinghy raft-up," said Karen as we headed back to *Pleasure* for cards.

*Dowry Creek*

# *The Army Base*

*N*ever in our wildest dreams did we expect to spend a night on an army base when we started the trip. We were in Beaufort, N.C., planning our next day's travel. It was almost ninety miles between Beaufort and the next major stop, Wrightsville Beach, mostly through an army base. The distance was definitely too far to make in one day. There was an anchorage, however, at the halfway point in the middle of the base. The army allowed cruisers to anchor overnight in a dredged basin at Mile Hammond, if there were no maneuvers going on. One had to listen on the VHF radio when nearing the base to hear if the army had closed the waterway. There was not a lot of choice - in fact, no choice. Mile Hammond it would be.

We left early.  The anchorage was forty-three miles away and we wanted to get a good spot at the "inn".  We knew a lot of other boats in Beaufort were planning to do the same run.  Everyone had to stop at Mile Hammond.

It was an interesting motor through the army base that day.  Where else could one see burned out hulks of tanks and personnel carriers in North America?  The guidebook stated that the army closed the canal when doing live fire exercises as they shot at targets on the ocean side of the canal.  It looked like they hit those targets.  *Vagus* made good time and arrived at the Mile Hammond anchorage about 3:00pm.  We motored through a short entrance into a small basin.  Only half a dozen sailboats and a large amphibian naval vessel, docked directly opposite the entrance off the canal, were in the basin when *Vagus* arrived.  We picked a spot off to the side, outside the channel to the dock.  After we completed our personal anchoring dance, we sat back for the rest of the afternoon.  The Army was loading the amphibian.  For the next few hours, tanks drove onto the amphibian and moved about, balancing the craft.  Someone with a loudspeaker directed traffic.  It was interesting viewing, watching both the amphibian and the anchorage fill up.  For the rest of the afternoon, a steady stream of boats came in to anchor.  We would have called it full after the first hour, but boats still kept coming; big ones and small ones, trawlers and sailboats.  Fortunately, the forecast called for no wind that night.  A good thing, as the boats were anchoring closer and closer together.  Soon, boats were as close as if they were on moorings.  There was no other place else to go.  They had to anchor here.

Around dinnertime, the skipper of the amphibian announced that they would be leaving at 5:00am and would require a clear channel to the entrance.  Soon after, a U.S. flagged boat came in and anchored right in the middle of the channel to the amphibian, directly in front of *Vagus*.  As soon as they had dropped their hook, another boat anchored behind the first boat.  I, who had met the skipper in Beaufort, went to *Vagus'* bow and called over to warn him about the announcement.

"The amphibian is leaving early and needs a clear channel to the entrance," I yelled.

"I'm a taxpayer," the skipper responded rather tiredly after a long day. "I pay their salary. They can just go around me."

It was not a typical Canadian response. I, a bit surprised, shrugged my shoulders.

"Okay," I said, and returned to the cockpit. Dusk was approaching. "Time to take down our Canadian flag anyway," I thought. "Maybe we will look like taxpayers as well." Through the evening, we sat in the cockpit with our after dinner tea and watched as boats kept coming in. There was no hope of escape; boats were anchored right out the channel into the waterway.

"It should be an interesting morning when the amphibian tries to leave," I commented to Karen as we prepared for bed.

At 5:00am, a large diesel engine started up and ran at a high idle speed. It was not a very quiet diesel. I arose from bed and sat in the companionway, looking out. I did not want to miss this for the world. At 5:30am, the amphibian's horn blared, giving the proper blasts for getting underway. I looked around. No boat lights were on. The tightly packed anchorage still slept. There was no way a vessel of that size could thread its way through all these anchored boats to the channel! And it appeared that no one was going to get out of the way. With a roar of its engine, the amphibian pulled away from the dock. I watched as searchlights from the amphibian played over the basin and the boats. The vessel appeared to be coming right at us. I was just starting to get worried when, suddenly, the amphibian veered off to the side of the basin and proceeded to motor along the basin edge, behind all the anchored boats. I knew the water was shallow there, too shallow for *Vagus*, but this was an amphibian. It passed within seven meters astern of *Vagus*, large searchlights keeping track of boats as it passed, and proceeded calmly out into the waterway. They had gotten out. I was amazed and gave the skipper full marks. There were still no lights on the other anchored boats. It appeared everyone else still slept. "Taxpayers here have impressive rights," I thought, as I headed back to a warm bed.

# *Colds Aren't Fun*

*I* caught a cold.  I was not sure where or how but, on leaving Mile Hammond, I started to feel it coming on.  It felt like a real good, old-fashioned, head cold.  My head felt all woolly inside and my thoughts seem to take a long time to become action.  My throat started to hurt and my nose, deciding to take a bit of a holiday, closed up shop and would not let anything pass in any direction.  I sat on my perch steering where Karen told me to go.  She was good at that.  Karen fed me liquids and pills, making all the appropriate noises that sick people hear from non-sick people.  I knew Karen would be a great nurse for three days.  After three days, she would get bored with the nursing routine.  She would feel that I really should be better in that amount of time anyway.  I knew the countdown was on.  Day one had started.

We pulled into Wrightsville Beach and had an awful anchoring. Although there was plenty of room, there was a current that my brain refused to acknowledge.  No matter what I seemed to do, *Vagus* kept drifting down on the same two boats.  After the third try, one of skippers, a Seven Seas Commodore from his cruising flag, unhelpfully yelled to anchor somewhere else, shaking his head and fist.  As *Vagus* moved away, another couple, seeing our plight, called over and recommended a good spot to anchor.  Karen motored to the recommended spot and, realizing I was in no shape for any serious decisions, told me to drop the anchor.  Karen set the anchor and we were in for the night.

We took the dinghy to shore and walked over to the beach for a quick look around.  At least, I have seen the pictures that Karen took of me standing on sand with people on surfboards in the background.  The cold medicine had definitely kicked in and my brain was no longer open for messages.

*Wrightsville Beach*

While I don't remember the beach, I do remember waking up the next morning. I thought that I felt better. I even told Karen that I was alright to go. We were underway by the time my body realized what was going on and made it known that it was not a good idea. Karen found a marina at St. James that we could duck into for the night. I missed the dock. Normally, missing the dock when docking a boat is a good thing. One does not want to hit the dock; one wants to come neatly alongside it. I, unfortunately, brought *Vagus* in too far from the dock. As there was not a boat in the slip beside us, we filled both dock areas and Karen could not get off the boat. This was in a marina with no current and no wind. I was definitely not in top form. The attendant was understanding, being new on the job, and helped us reposition *Vagus* properly alongside the slip. Bicycles were available at the marina office as the shower building was so far away. Exercise is supposed to help a cold. After a good long hot shower, Karen fixed dinner and I went to bed.

I woke up the next morning and noted it was day three of my allotted sick time. Now to be aware of this fact was an improvement. I must be getting better. We worked out a strategy. I would drive the boat wherever Karen told me to. That was it. That was the strategy. Karen would do everything else. I would put my total energies on keeping the boat in the middle of the channel and going from marker to marker. I thought that I could just barely handle that. We made 54 miles that day. I did not move; I was in a different world; I just drove. Karen kept me fed and watered, and told me where to go. It was a long day. Longer than we would have liked but there were no convenient stops along the way.

*Cold Jim*

We decided to stop at another marina, as I was not up for anchoring. Karen picked Osprey Marina, a new marina just off the ICW. This part of the ICW is in a bayou. Trees, hung heavily with moss and vines, rose from black water on both sides. Karen loved it. The entrance channel to the marina was impossible to see from the waterway, however, until *Vagus* was right beside it. We first spotted a small sign with an arrow and the word "Osprey", tacked to a tree at the water's edge. As we got to the sign, it pointed down a 15-meter wide, tree-lined lane way. I turned *Vagus* down the lane as Karen radioed in. Two dock attendants came out to take the lines. It was dead calm in the marina - they must have heard about the last docking I had done. When we registered, the marina attendant gave us a gift basket full of cheese, crackers, Danishes and other assorted goodies. We felt welcome. The marina advertised itself as a hurricane hole and it certainly would be a good one. It was a small basin in the wilderness, full of friendly people. I was starting to feel human. Just as well, for tomorrow was day four. Karen, as nurse, would be off duty.

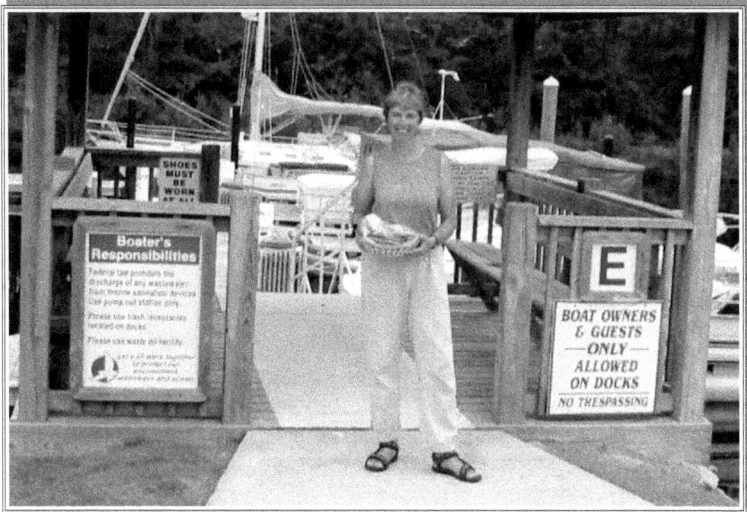

*Gift basket from Osprey Marina*

# The Propane Expedition

*W*e needed propane. There were lots of places to get propane but no one would fill our tanks. Although Vagus' propane tanks were brand new when we left, the U.S. had brought in a new law requiring all propane tanks to have a special overfill protection device. Tanks with this device were not at the time available in Canada. On top of that, the propane tank lockers on Vagus only fit a 10 pound tank of one manufacturer's design. The whole boat appeared to be designed around these tanks. We searched through Annapolis and around the boat show for a tank. Armed with the locker dimensions carefully scribed in my notebook and a tape measure in my hand, I checked with every chandler, measuring every tank in sight. I even looked at the expensive aluminum tanks that required a small mortgage to purchase. Nothing fit the locker. We were starting to get low on propane.

The propane situation was getting critical by the time we reached Beaufort, North Carolina. While exploring Beaufort, we spotted a store that sold barbeques and barbeque supplies. We went in and explained our plight to a sympathetic sales lady. Overfill devices could be installed in older propane tanks, she said, but they did not have the one for the smaller 10 pound tank in stock. They could get one in a few days, she offered. We were planning to leave the next day. As we turned to go, the lady asked, "What direction are you going - north or south?"

"South," I replied.

"Well," she said, "You are in luck. South Carolina has appealed the law and it is now in the courts. Your tanks can legally be filled in South Carolina."

We thanked the lady and left with much happier faces. South Carolina was the next State on our journey.

With propane high on the "To Do" list, we headed for Georgetown, South Carolina. Georgetown is a major sport fishing center and there is a good entrance to the ocean by the town. As it is also a fair sized town, we thought that we should be able to get both tanks filled. Finding the anchorage by the town center crowded with both permanently moored and transient boats, we headed for the marina. The marina appeared to be a good walk from the downtown but we thought it would be nice to stretch our legs. While checking in, we asked for directions to the nearest propane filling station. It was on the other side of town, about as far away from the marina as one could walk and still be in Georgetown.

Being the optimist, I said "Let's walk there with the tanks. We can explore and have lunch in the downtown area while the tanks are being filled, then take a taxi back with the full tanks." It sounded like an awful lot of walking to Karen. She thought maybe we should take a taxi both ways. I confidently pulled out the map that the marina office had given me.

"It's no problem," I stated emphatically, waving the map in Karen's face. "We just follow this street, make a turn here and there, and there we are!"

I sounded so positive, she agreed. She will always remember agreeing.

We closed up Vagus and off we went - backpacks on and me with a propane bottle in each hand. The marina drawing of the town layout was a copy of a hand-made sketch. It was not to scale. It was done by someone who started out drawing the streets around the marina carefully, and then realized that there would not be room on the paper to fill in the rest of the city. The artist managed to get all the streets on the paper by using a variable compression ratio, which only the artist knew. The streets and street names were there. Distances were guesswork. It turned out to be a long walk. It was hot and it was getting near lunch time. We found the propane fill station at the side of a garage and convenience store in the rougher part of the city, an area where everything was behind black iron bars and padlocks. The attendant said, "The guy that fills the tanks will be back in an hour."

I looked around. I pulled out my map.

"Look," I showed Karen, who was resting by the tanks in the shade. "We just have to go down this street, hang a left and we are in the downtown area by the channel. We can still pop down there for lunch while the tanks are filled and pick them up later." I tend to use words like "pop" and "flit" and "no problem" when I am trying to convince Karen about how easy something is. I really had no idea of the distances involved but to Karen it sounded a lot better than sitting outside a garage in this part of town for an hour.

We entrusted the tanks to the attendant, who immediately locked them in a compound with other rusty propane tanks. "Not a good sign," I thought. I only mentioned to Karen that they were locked in a secure area.

Karen replied, "That's good, because without tanks, we can't cook."

We set out – me, with an uneasy feeling in my stomach, leading the way. We walked and we walked, unknowingly missing a critical left turn. We were now walking by a steel plant. I looked at the map and confidently stated that the left turn must be after the plant. Steel plants, by their nature, are big. It took a long time to walk to the other side. And the walk was not nice. It was along a narrow, cracked sidewalk, beside a busy, dusty road. Industrial truck traffic roared past, blowing dirt and exhaust in our faces. Karen's foot started to hurt - a blister was developing on her heel. Finally, we reached the other side of the plant and turned left. The road dead-ended at another industrial company. I was bewildered. I stopped a pickup truck to ask the driver for directions, showing my out-of-scale map. The driver said, "You're really lost, man! You should have turned on the road before the steel plant." Karen started muttering; I was speechless. We had already been gone an hour from the service station.

"I'm going back to the propane before we get further lost," she declared as she limped back up the street by the steel plant. I walked very quietly behind her.

We finally reached the station. The propane tanks were ready. I paid for the propane fill, asked the attendant to call a taxi, and sat down beside the tanks to wait. Very shortly, I could smell propane. Propane was leaking out the high pressure release vent from one of the tanks. I called the attendant. The attendant laughed. "I probably filled that one a little full!" He grabbed the tank and went around the corner to bleed off some propane and reduce the pressure. The day was really not going well. Just then the taxi pulled up. It was 2:00 as we headed back to the marina. We still had not eaten.

"At least we got the propane," I said in as cheerful voice as I could muster.

Karen remained silent.

# *The Mega Dock*

$W$e were looking forward to Charleston. While there, we planned to meet with J.P. and Colette and to explore the town. We had also arranged for an engine water pump to be shipped to the town marina. *Vagus'* pump had developed a copious leak and needed rebuilding. When we reached the marina, we were assigned a place along the inside of the main dock between two very wide catamarans. It was very tight. I brought *Vagus* in close, Karen threw the dock lines to the waiting attendants, and they pulled *Vagus* broadside into the dock.

"I guess we don't leave until one of those catamarans do," I said.

The dock attendants had ridden bikes to help us. I thought this strange until I got off the boat and looked down the dock. The dock was floating concrete, about 4 meters wide, and it went on out of sight. Several small Waterway cruise ships docked on the other side. Setting off for the marina office, it took me almost five minutes to get there at a good brisk walk. Of course the showers were by the office. J.P. and Colette got a nice slip in a part of the marina on the other side of the showers – a long walk from *Vagus*. It was, without a doubt, the longest dock that we had been on in our travels.

We had a great time visiting Charleston with J.P. and Colette, and catching up on their adventures since we last were together. We took a bus tour of the city, visited the market, and enjoyed She-crab soup. Somehow, as well, I found time to replace the water pump. All too soon the time came to go. I started to worry about how we would get out. The catamarans were not showing any signs of moving soon. And the current, changing with the tide, ran always parallel to the dock. I mulled the problem over. I would lie in bed and try to imagine the forces at work and how the forces would move *Vagus*. It usually was not in the direction I wanted. I sat in the cockpit and looked at the direction and speed of water flowing at about the time that I thought we would be leaving. Fortunately, we would be able to leave close to slack tide so the current should not be too much of a problem. I remembered write-ups in sailing magazines about getting off tricky docking situations. "This is about as tricky as it gets," I thought. Karen also knew that this exit was going to be a challenge.

"Are we going to be able to get out of here?" she asked.

"Still working on it," I muttered, thinking that anchoring was definitely easier and less stressful.

The day came to leave. The weather was good and once again there would be a mass exodus of boats heading south from Charleston. Everyone likes nice travel weather and all listen to the same weather forecast. I checked out of the marina and asked for assistance leaving. The staff was used to helping and told me to call when I was ready. An attendant would bike to our boat. I walked back. My heart was pounding. Something about doing a maneuver that I had never done before, and not hitting any of the expensive boats around us at the same time, got my adrenaline going. Like a football player at pre-game time, I started to psyche myself up.

"I have my plan and it will work." I got back to *Vagus*. Karen had finished getting everything ready to leave. I explained the whole plan. She didn't understand but I seemed positive.

"Just tell me what *I* have to do."

I explained her part again and called for the attendants. I checked the current. It was moving in the right direction at about the right speed. I took a couple of the large fenders and tied them at the bow. The attendant arrived and I told her the plan. We would first cast off the stern lines. I would turn the wheel so the current would swing *Vagus'* stern out into the channel. The snubbed bowline would keep the boat from moving forward and *Vagus* should move perpendicular to the dock, with the bow in and the fenders keeping the bow from hitting the dock. As I applied reverse, the attendant should remove the bowline, toss it to Karen, and we would back out and turn around in the channel.

The stern line came off and the stern slowly moved out from the dock as predicted. Just as the stern cleared the catamaran in front of us, I looked down the channel. Another sailboat had just left its slip and was coming at full speed towards us down the channel! If *Vagus* backed out now, there would not be room for both boats in the channel at the same time. The other boat was not stopping.

I yelled, "Hold off on releasing the bow line!" and continued to let *Vagus* slowly pivot out from the dock. Timing was critical. "If the rotation is slow enough and the other boat fast enough," I thought, "we can still do it." I tried to judge the distances. Now I hoped the other boat would not slacken speed. The other boat got near; the attendant was starting to look worried; I called to release the bowline. Karen quickly pulled in the line and headed for the cockpit just as the other boat steamed by *Vagus'* stern. The skipper did not even notice *Vagus*. As the other boat went by, I put *Vagus* in reverse, pulled neatly into the channel, turned around, waved at the attendant, and proceeded out. I could breathe again. We had done it. It was just the start to another day of cruising.

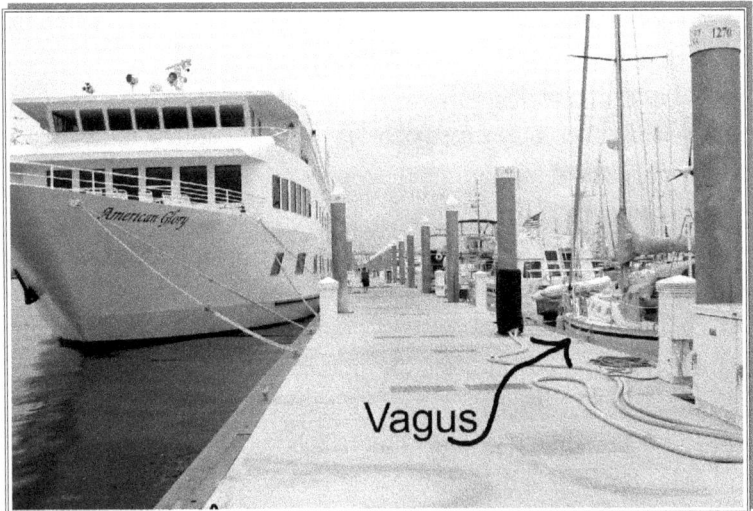

*Mega dock, Charleston, SC*

# *Grassland Anchoring*

*I*t was strange traveling through the grasslands of Georgia. The area is flat and full of grass growing well over three meters tall. The ICW follows meandering creeks that snake through the grasslands. These creeks are full of twists, turns, ox bows and every sort of change in direction one could imagine. When I looked out, I only could see a bit of creek ending in grass indicating, I hoped, the next turn. In the distance, I could see masts of other sailboats, sticking proudly above the tall grass, ahead of *Vagus*. As I watched, the masts would move in one direction, then another, then, sometimes, crisscross in front of us. It was truly a strange sight.

To anchor at night, we would move off the main creek to a side channel and follow the channel a short distance to a suitable spot. Other boats did the same until, in a short while, masts stuck out of the grass at different spots all around us, like tall trees on the prairies.

The only downside to the grasslands was the no-see-ums. These very small biting flies could easily crawl through normal mosquito netting. And their bite was inversely proportional to their size. It really hurt when they took a chunk out of one. We had arrived late in the day at Buckhead Creek. J.P. and Colette were already anchored and J.P. was setting up his barbeque on the stern rail. We waved as we passed *Safina* and motored a little further up the stream to anchor. Dusk was approaching as we finished anchoring.

"I think it will be too dark to barbeque," I suggested. "Let's just fix something below for dinner." As I went below, I happened to glance over at J.P.. J.P. was dancing around and waving his arms in his cockpit. His barbeque was smoking. "J.P. must be playing something really upbeat on his stereo," I thought. "He must be feeling particularly good tonight!" Then the first no-see-um struck.

"No-see-ums!" I yelled to Karen. No-see-ums are particularly vicious at dusk. They were also hungry after a long day. Karen dove into the quarter berth and pulled out the no-see-um screens for the companionway. Passing the screen to me, she went to shut the other hatches. I carefully placed the screen over the companionway opening, making sure to cover every available opening, completing the job from below. The no-see-um screen was specially made for us and had an extremely fine hole size. It was so fine that air barely got through, but it worked. In the past, on Lake Ontario, we had sat below and watched no-see-ums walk through regular mosquito screens. This was not going to happen here. So, with relatively few bites, we were secure below.

We called on the radio to *Safina*. "What music are you dancing to in your cockpit?"

"No music, just a buzz in my head," he replied.

*Safina* did not have no-see-um screens and their companionway had been open the whole time. There were no-see-ums below as well as in the cockpit. They had smelled dinner.

J.P. went on further, "I guess we will be rocking and rolling all night!" I thought I had better leave that comment alone.

# *Dolphins*

*O*ne of the best treats in traveling the waterway was seeing dolphins. Dolphins are interesting, exciting mammals. As we motored along, dolphins would see *Vagus* and come over to play. They would usually come up to the bow, riding and jumping in the bow wake. It looked like the boat would run over them but the dolphins seemed to enjoy this high-speed game of tag and always got out of the way. Another cruiser had told Karen, "Dolphins like to be waved at and talked to. This encourages them to visit your boat." So, whenever I spotted some dolphins, I would call to Karen and point in the dolphin direction. Karen would drop whatever she was doing, hurry to the bow, waving her arms and calling in her "dolphin talk". I thought it sounded awfully close to baby talk. I was not sure that this routine actually worked, but Karen was convinced. It did draw some curious looks from people on the shore though.

One evening as we lay at anchor in Delaroche Creek, I spotted some activity near *Vagus* along the muddy shoreline. On the edge of the creek, there was a small beach of black, slippery mud, next to tall grass. Four or five dolphins were frolicking in the water near the beach. The dolphins were taking turns beaching themselves on the muddy beach, rolling about, and then sliding back into the water. Sometimes several would beach together and roll about. I thought that it looked like they were having great fun. I suggested to Karen that we go try the beach too.

"I don't think so, Jim," said Karen.

*Dolphin playing with Vagus*

I had an encounter with a dolphin "of the close kind". I was on my perch and it was early afternoon. The steering was not demanding, as the channel was wide. It was warm and we had just finished lunch. It was one of those lazy, hazy days when all was right with the world. I felt very mellow. I wandered off into the dream world where I lived during long stretches behind the wheel. Little did I know that a dolphin had spotted me. I had not spotted the dolphin. The dolphin quietly approached *Vagus* from the stern quarter. Suddenly, the dolphin leaped high out of the water right beside me. At that particular moment in time, I happened to notice something out of the corner of my eye. I turned my head and looked directly at a dolphin in mid-air. The dolphin looked back and squeaked. Now, I am famous for my startle reflex, and I was well and thoroughly startled. I didn't just jump. I yelled and leaped to the other side of the cockpit, my perch collapsing into a jumble of cockpit cushions, as the dolphin gracefully dove back into the water. I could feel my heart pounding - a good thing, I thought. Karen came running to the companionway.

"What happened?" I was still speechless; I just stood and pointed. The dolphin, still swimming alongside the boat, rolled over on its side and looked up at me with one eye. To this day I swear I could hear the dolphin making a laughing sound.

## *The Earring*

*I* had thought about getting an earring before we left home. "All good pirates have earrings," I thought. It would make me distinctive. It was a statement. There is also an important practical reason for getting an earring. An earring is supposed to improve distance vision. Every good pirate knew that. The ear lobe is apparently an acupuncture point that is related to vision. So I could justify it. What I could not do was get up the nerve to get my ear pierced. The thought of going into a jewelry store and having an eighteen year old sales clerk punch a hole in my ear lobe made me shudder. I could just hear the clerks giggling later at lunch about punching a hole in the ear of this old guy and the guy fainting dead away. Ears, I felt, were not meant for holes to be punched in. They should come with the proper attachment points for earrings.

One day as I walked by a jewelry store at a local mall, I noticed a sign in front of the store - "Free Ear Piercing With Purchase of Earrings". There was a table set up in the center of the store. The table had a white cloth on it and a girl, with a nice white lab coat on, sat purposefully on a chair. She looked eighteen. She had nice makeup on; in fact, she had a lot of nice makeup on. I wondered how they pierced ears. I had never told Karen my interest. I thought she might giggle. So I had never asked her how her ears had been pierced. I thought that they might use something like a hole punch. That would be how I would do it. I would just walk in and the girl would put the hole punch around my ear lobe. One punch and it was done. I wondered what they did with the little punched-out bits. Maybe there was a bucket under the table with ice in it where they threw the little ear plugs for disposal at the end of the day. Maybe the girl was paid by the number of plugs she had at day's end. I bent over as I walked past, trying to look under the table. There was a waste paper basket but no bucket. The girl shifted in her seat, crossed her legs, and started to glare at me. I moved on. "How do they do it?" I again wondered.

Karen would not find out my interest until we were at Chesapeake City. By this time, I had seen a lot of guys with an earring. In fact, most male sailors that we met had earrings. It was not unique or distinctive; it was common. I was disappointed. Part of the reason was gone. We were standing on the dock talking to J.P. and Colette. George from *SeaWalk*, the boat we had all shared an anchorage with at Breakwater Harbour, had just left. George had an earring. In fact he had several - and a toe ring, and purple painted toenails. This was escalation.

J.P. is one of the few sailors that he had met that did not have an earring. I asked him.

"No!" J.P. exclaimed emphatically. "I'll never get an earring."

"Well," I said. "What about a toe ring then? Nothing has to get pierced for a toe ring."

We had a good laugh. J.P. was dead set against any adornments.

Later, when we were alone, Karen asked me if I was interested in getting an earring. I confessed. "Maybe, but I'm worried about the whole act of piercing." I shared my hole punch theory on how I thought it would be done. Karen didn't just giggle. She laughed.

We were in St. Augustine, Florida, when the subject of an earring came up again. Once again we had met up with J.P. and Colette, and were planning to meet for Happy Hour later in the day. As it was nearing Christmas, we were looking for small gifts. Everything must be small to fit on a boat. In one store, I spotted a pair of stick-on earrings that looked exactly like pierced earrings when on. I could not resist. We made sure that we got back to our boat without being seen by J.P. or Colette. Karen helped me put on the earring. "It looks good," I thought as we left to meet J.P. and Colette. We were still walking down the dock, about ten meters from J.P., when we could see J.P.'s mouth suddenly drop.

"What did you do?" he yelled.

"Thought I'd get my ear pierced," I replied proudly, turning my head to the side so J.P. could get a good look.

J.P. stared speechlessly at my ear. I told him how they had used a little hole punch and asked if he wanted to see my ear plug. J.P. started to laugh – he knew when his ear was being pulled.

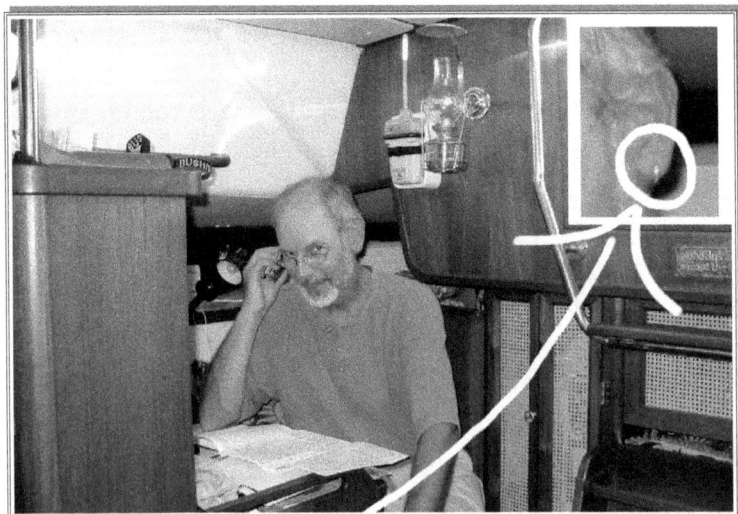

*Check out the earring!*

# *The Pelican Tree*

*W*e were finally in Florida.  As we motored south, the weather had got warmer.  It was wonderful to feel the sun after all those days bundled in cold weather clothes and rain gear.  We were on our way to Stuart where we would meet some friends and get sorted out before going to the Bahamas.  Our trip along the ICW neared an end.

"We've done well!" we thought.  We had never run hard aground.  Although we were sure that we had left some furrows in the soft ICW mud, we had never come to a complete stop.  Furrows don't count as groundings.  We would treat ourselves. We would stop at a marina at Fort Pierce and go out for dinner.  We pulled down the channel to the marina and were told to pull alongside the main dock in the channel.

"Well, that should be an easy exit in the morning," I thought.  As we pulled in, we saw a boat listing to one side at the dock.  But all I could think about was a hot shower and a cold beer at the bar.  We pulled alongside the dock.  The dock was high - really high.

"How am I going to get off the boat?" asked Karen.  "Oh – I see – there are footholds on the pylons to climb up."  This statement prompted me to glance at the depth sounder.  Normally I always asked about the depth before going into a marina.  The desire for a shower and beer had made me forget this rule.  The depth sounder read five feet.

I called the attendant over,  "When is low tide?"

"We're at low tide, Skip," came the reply.

I breathed a sigh of relief.

"And don't worry.  The bottom is soft mud."

I now remembered seeing the listing boat on the way in.  Although Karen was still concerned, I could feel the shower and taste the cold beer.

"We'll be fine," I said calmly, hoping I was right.  I rocked the boat.  It was still moving and this was supposed to be as low as the tide would get.  We cleaned up then headed for the restaurant.  We sat on the balcony overlooking the marina and the waterway, Jimmy Buffet playing in the background.  The beer was cold and the dinner hot.  We watched the sunset, reminiscing about our travels. As we returned to *Vagus*, we were reminded the adventure never ends.

After negotiating the climb down to the deck, Karen pointed. "Look at that tree at the end of the harbour!" The tree was full of large objects that were not there when we left. We got the binoculars. The objects were pelicans. We were looking at our first pelican tree. Hundreds of pelicans had come to sleep for the night in this particular tree. It was magical.

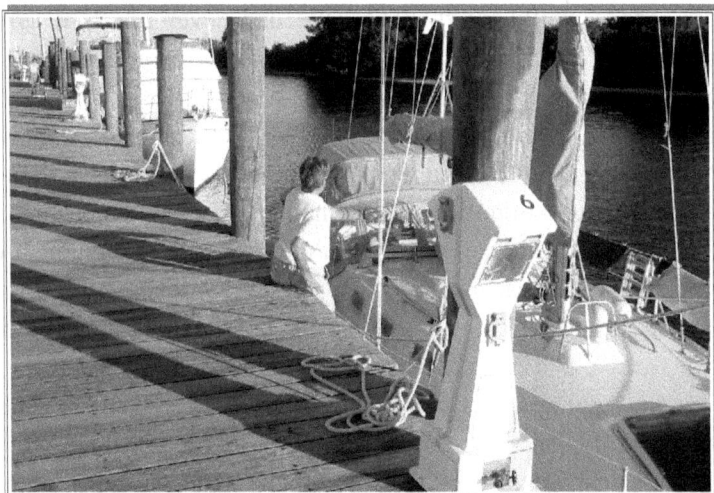

*Getting off or getting on?*

# Florida

Stuart, Florida, to Lucaya, Grand Bahama Island

# 21. Hanging Out

$A$s we motored to the mooring ball in Stuart, the marina manager waited in a little boat to pass the mooring line. It was the last mooring left. The manager knew we were coming and had saved it for us. J.P. and Colette had arrived the day before and made sure the manager knew we were coming.

He told J.P. and Colette, "*Vagus* had better hurry up. I can't hold the mooring for long."

But we made it. It was almost the end of our trip along the ICW. *Vagus* had been traveling the ditch for almost five weeks and we were looking forward to stopping in one spot for a while. Friends who had traveled the ICW the previous year had recommended this marina to us. Stuart is a staging ground for boats planning to go to the Bahamas. The plan was to take a break, install solar panels that we had ordered to be delivered to the marina, get the boat surveyed for our new insurance policy, and do a major provisioning in preparation for the trip to the Bahamas. J.P. and Colette were leaving the next day to continue south on their way to Cuba. But we were looking forward to stopping. About 50 boats floated on moorings at the marina. The office had great showers and laundry facilities and, as well, shopping and several good restaurants were conveniently nearby. The spot looked good.

# *The Survey*

$F$irst order of business was the survey. We had already contracted a local Marine Surveyor, Russ, to do the insurance survey. Our new policy required a survey before they would cover us throughout the Caribbean Sea. The friends who had recommended the Stuart marina had also recommended Russ, a sailor who lived on one of the moorings. Russ told us to meet him at the marina dock first thing the following morning. Early the next day, we slipped our mooring lines and headed for the marina dock. Russ was standing on the dock as promised. He had a video camera and starting going through the boat, recording and talking as he went. He asked questions. I felt like it was an exam. I had rebuilt or upgraded most of the systems on the boat. I was proud of the changes but did not know how they would pass inspection. Russ made me unload lockers. Russ then crawled inside the lockers, still filming and talking. He started an inventory list. He took down serial numbers. Finally, near noon, Russ sat down.

"Okay," he said. "What have I missed?"

He then went back over most of the boat.

"Looks good," he finally declared. "I'll get it written up and go over it with you next Monday. I may have a few more questions in the meantime."

I was exhausted. I still had to put everything away.

Russ returned on Monday as promised. I was nervous. Russ motored out to *Vagus* in his dinghy and came aboard. He handed me a large yellow envelope. Carefully, I opened the seal and pulled out a blue folder, filled with a 20-page document all about *Vagus*. There were even colour pictures highlighting things that Russ had seen as he went through his inspection. Russ had been impressed. His summary stated *Vagus* was in "Bristol" condition; a term he had only used a few times in his survey career. There were a few changes to make but they were minor. I felt relieved - *Vagus* had passed. All the work during the cold Canadian springs had paid off. *Vagus* was in great condition and a boat, according to Russ, that one could take anywhere. And Russ had a lot of sea miles under his belt. As we sat, Karen gave Russ a coffee and he talked about his sailing days. Russ used to leave from Miami, sail directly across to Nassau in the Bahamas, anchor long enough to buy several rum cakes – "You have to get rum cakes in Nassau – they're the best!" he declared – then head offshore to the Virgin Islands.

"You have to keep north and out of the trade winds to make the Virgins," he said.

We shared our thoughts and plans. We mentioned our wish to try an offshore sail but we were also concerned about the reality.

"With a boat like this, you will have no problem," stated Russ. "Offshore is easier than doing the island-hopping route, trying to dodge all those hard edges. Besides, it is beautiful and peaceful riding the waves. You'll love it."

The time went quickly and Russ had to leave. He climbed back in his dinghy and made off to his next appointment. I sat back in the cockpit. "Bristol Condition," I thought. It was nice hearing that from someone else.

## *Solar Panels*

*W*ith the survey out of the way, I could focus on the solar panels. We had ordered the panels to provide some quiet energy to our batteries while anchored out in the sunny south. At least that was the idea. The solar panels were supposed to be at the marina office when we arrived. They were not. They did not come during the first week. I called the supplier.

"They're not there?" said the supplier. "Well, they should be there any day now."

After three days, I called back. The supplier promised to check into it and call back. He called back later that day.

"There's been a mistake," he said. "The panels are not coming. We misplaced the order and they haven't been ordered yet. We can place the order today but they will take another week for delivery as they come from New York."

I was not amused; I felt between a rock and a hard place.

"We wanted to go to the Bahamas for Christmas. It is already the end of the first week in December and we need those panels." The phone receiver was firmly clenched in my hand.

The supplier was apologetic and promised the panels would definitely be there by the following Friday.

I went back to *Vagus* to tell Karen. By now, the whole anchorage knew the solar panel story. A boater on one of the moorings ran a little coffee bar at the marina. The lunches and coffee were delicious and it had become the local hangout for finding out what was going on. Whenever a delivery came to the marina, anyone seeing one of us would say, "I thought I saw your panels in the office." I made many false trips to the office.

The following Wednesday the panels arrived – early! The marina manager had radioed the news. By the time we reached the office, we had been told three times by three different sets of people that our panels were in. Checking the boxes at the office, I was relieved to find they were the right panels. Finally they were here – two large cardboard boxes containing our precious solar panels. We carried the panels down to the dinghy. They looked a lot larger in real life than I had imagined.

"How will I get the panels and Karen all in the dinghy?" I pondered, looking at the panels, Karen and the dinghy. We brought the dinghy alongside the dock and somehow manhandled the panels into the dinghy. The panels took up the whole dinghy. I barely squeezed in by the motor.

"Now, what about Karen?" I thought.

Karen thought the same thing. "I'll just sit on the bow," she said as she carefully climbed in and perched herself on the bow tube of our inflatable dinghy.

Off we went - Karen precariously sitting on the bow, two very expensive solar panels balanced between the side tubes, and me squeezed by the motor. I went very slowly. It felt like a very long trip back to *Vagus*. We made it without anything or anyone getting wet. Sometimes one just gets lucky.

"Now, how to get the panels from the dinghy to *Vagus* without dropping the panels in the water?"

Karen climbed off first and tied the bow and stern of the dinghy to *Vagus*. I carefully slid a panel below the lifelines as Karen grabbed and pulled it onto the deck. I wondered how single-handers manage this lifestyle.

We were excited. Karen got a knife to open the packaging and I started slicing. I got one end open. The panels were surrounded by little Styrofoam packaging noodles. It was windy. Suddenly, as I looked in the box for the panel, the noodles made their escape in a gust of wind, scattering over the water. Rapidly, Styrofoam noodles surrounded *Vagus*, gently floating away. I hastily closed the box.

Karen said, "We have to pick those up. We can't let them get away."

We climbed back into the dinghy. The next hour was spent roaring around the anchorage, Karen hanging over the side, scooping up noodles. People came on deck to watch. They thought it was a new dinghy game. They wondered if they could join in.

Finally, it was back to the solar panels. The panels turned out to be easy to install on the side rails. The hard part was the wiring. One panel was to be installed on each side of the boat so both cockpit lockers had to be emptied and redistributed around the boat before I could run the wires. Karen claimed a spot on the settee and, with a book, settled in for a long siege. After much muttering, and, surprisingly, no bandages, I finished. I started to clean up. It was now dark so I did not know if the panels worked but at least they were installed.

The panels did not work. The next morning, I excitedly got up to check on the panels. Only one panel was working. It was a sad breakfast. Karen grabbed her book. She knew I could not leave a problem alone. We could be in Stuart until the end of time or until I fixed the panel, whichever came first. The problem turned out to be simple incomplete connection. Within an hour, healthy amps from both panels were flowing into *Vagus'* batteries. It was time for another cup of coffee.

*Dinghy dock at Stuart, FL*

# *Christmas*

*A* suitable weather window to cross to the Bahamas was not happening. Mid-December had arrived and, with no window apparent for more than a week, we decided to stay in Stuart for Christmas. With that decision, we could relax our weather watch and let our son, Alex, know. He had said he would drive down to Stuart if we were still there.

By this time, we had been traveling by boat for over four months. Alex took two days by car to get the same distance South. Nobody said boat travel was fast.

It was our first Christmas away from home and family. We were feeling lonely and Alex's arrival really cheered us up. Karen had decorated the boat, turning the mast into a Christmas mast. Garland strings were woven along the hand rails below. *Vagus* had taken on a festive air. Alex brought presents from Jeff and Caitilin as well as a vinaterta – a traditional Icelandic Christmas cake – from my Mom. It would not be Christmas without one. Alex also was able to bring a special computer monitor cable so we could better use our monitor to watch movies. We had not been able to find one in Stuart. The last few days had been spent buying little gifts for each other. A big potluck Christmas dinner was planned at the marina office for all the boats in the anchorage. But there is nothing like having family visit.

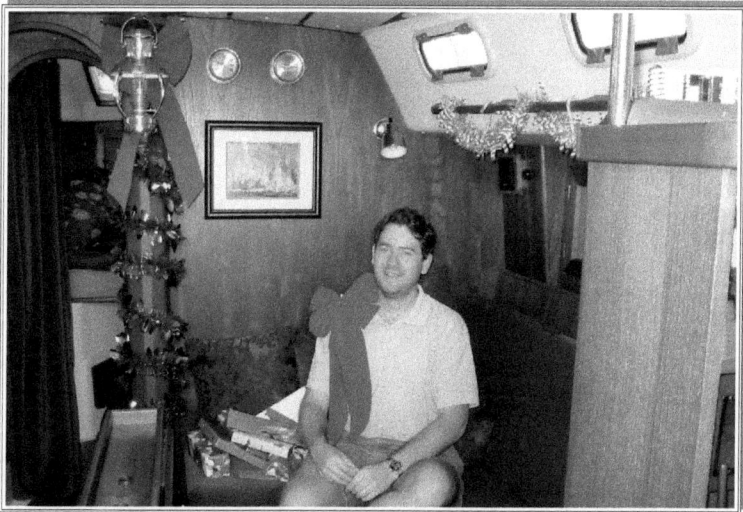

*Our best Christmas present!*

On Christmas morning, we opened the presents that had found their way to the mast tree, then made calls to family in Canada. In the afternoon was the potluck. Over 30 people from the boats on the moorings met for the outdoor Christmas meal. We were amazed at what people can cook in a small boat stove. Someone had even cooked a large turkey, complete with stuffing. At dusk, full and happy, we returned to *Vagus* for a movie.

We had promised Alex some beach time. On Boxing Day, Alex

drove us to the ocean at Bathtub Beach on Hutchinson Island. It was a bit windy and cool but Alex still managed to get in the water for a short snorkel. It was a fun time, including a tailgate picnic at Alex's truck. All too soon, it was over. Alex had to head back north to work. We loaded Alex's truck with our winter clothes for him to take back as we hoped we were through with winter. It was sad to see Alex leave but it was time to move on. It looked like a weather window might be opening in the next week.

# 22. The Crossing

$T$he weather forecast indicated a possible window for crossing the Gulf Stream opening in four days. Alex had just left for home so we scurried around to complete the final provisioning for the Bahamas. Provisioning was a bit of a production. To get to the grocery store, we took our dinghy up a small creek near the end of the moorings. Up this creek was a park that had a dock where we could lock the dinghy. A ten-minute walk along a busy road then brought us to the grocery store. The store manager was very accommodating and allowed cruisers to take their groceries in store shopping carts back to the dinghy dock - as long as they returned the carts. So we would walk to the store, do our shopping, and then, pushing two full shopping carts, walk back along US 1 Highway to the dinghy. After loading the dinghy, I returned the carts while Karen watched over the supplies. Hoping Karen would still be there when I got back, I would enjoy the walk back with no encumbrances. We then motored, with a very full dinghy, out to *Vagus*. It was fun trying to unload bags of groceries from a bouncing dinghy into a bouncing boat, each bouncing to its own unique pattern, without dropping anything overboard. The rest of the day was spent entertaining ourselves with the game of "where can I stash this item and still find it in the future?" Fortunately, Karen got into the spirit of making lists and made inventories of the foodstuffs as they were squirreled away in each bin.

One of the most important items in provisioning was beer. We had heard that beer cost over forty dollars a case in the Bahamas. It was considerably cheaper in the U.S.! But beer cans take up a lot of room and we were limited in what we could take. Just before we left, Karen, while cleaning the fridge, noticed an area under a shelf at the bottom of our fridge that was not being used. It looked like an excellent, long-term storage spot. Karen was always looking for "out of the way" spots to store things.

"Why don't we put beer cans in that area at the bottom of the fridge?" she called excitedly.

"Great idea," I said, taking an interest now that beer was involved.

We went out to buy more beer. When we were done, an extra four dozen cans of beer sat nicely cooling in the bottom of the fridge, ready for those sunny Bahamas days. *Vagus'* sat lower in the water with every trip to the store but, finally, we had everything we needed.

Saying goodbye to friends in the marina, we slipped the lines to the mooring in Stuart for the last time. We were on the way to Lake Worth. Lake Worth has a large protected area in which to anchor and wait for departure, about four miles from the Palm Beach inlet. This inlet is a Class A inlet into the ocean - big freighters routinely traverse it. We left early on a Monday morning. Although the trip was only 30 miles, we had to pass through seven bridges. It would be a long day. Part way to Lake Worth, Karen spotted Daydream motoring the other way. We had met Joe and Lisa on *Daydream* at the Thanksgiving potluck dinner in Stuart. *Daydream* was on a mooring near us and had left before Christmas to cross to the Bahamas. I had seen the same weather window but, by that time, Alex was on his way. Besides, I had felt the window was a little too short for a crossing.

Playfully we called to *Daydream* as they motored past, "Hey, *Daydream*! You are going the wrong way!"

They responded, not so playfully, continuing up the channel, "Yes, we had a confrontation with the Gulf Stream and we are going back to Canada."

We were stunned. *Daydream* had made the crossing several times before. They were experienced and, in conversation at Thanksgiving, had boasted how they liked to sail in lots of wind. I had thought that they were talking about more wind than I was comfortable with. Still, they had a beautiful, very seaworthy, forty-foot ketch. What had happened? The exchange did nothing to bolster our confidence. The

Gulf Stream has a bad reputation. The stream is actually a river in the ocean that runs north at high speeds along the Florida coast between Florida and the Bahamas. It is one of the most difficult and dangerous bodies of water that we would have to cross between Florida and the Southern Caribbean. Boats waited sometimes weeks to get the proper combination of wind and waves to cross. We had been told any wind with a north component would act against the stream to throw up sharp, steep sided waves which were, at best, uncomfortable and could be down right dangerous.

We arrived, somewhat shaken, at the Lake Worth anchorage about 3:00pm. The anchorage is a large lagoon, completely surrounded by houses and condos. The only way one can reach land is to motor a dinghy to a small bridge that crosses a side road, tie up to a branch by the bridge, and wade to the muddy bank. At least there is a grocery store near by, if needed. After anchoring and getting settled, we looked around. This anchorage is one of the main staging areas for boats crossing the Gulf Stream. Surely other boats anchored here would be planning to cross on the window tomorrow. Karen spotted a boat near us that looked like a cruiser and people were working on deck. They looked like they were getting ready to leave. Karen hopped in the dinghy and went over. Half an hour later she was back.

"How did it go? Are they going to the Bahamas?" I asked.

"No," said Karen. "They just got back. They went offshore from Norfolk, got blown in a storm down to the Bahamas, hated the Bahamas and are going back home."

It was not a tale we needed to hear. Now two boats were going home. We looked around again and could not see any other boats that looked like they were getting ready. I went to check the weather forecast again.

The weather forecast had not changed. From my limited understanding, it looked like a good window tomorrow - not ideal, but good enough. The winds were light but from the east, so it would probably be a motor sail across. The waves were also down. But we still could not figure out why other boats were not lined up to go. Had we missed something? After some soul searching, including once again questioning why we were doing this, we decided to give it a try. At the worst, we could turn around and head down to Miami where *Safina* had gone. We decided to leave at 5:00pm the next day and sail overnight directly to Lucaya on Grand Bahama Island, arriving about 9:00am the following morning. It was not an easy sleep that night.

The next day rose bright and clear as predicted. We still were not sure we were doing the right thing as we started the routine of getting *Vagus* ready for sea. Raising the dinghy to tie it down on deck, I discovered another job. Growth had accumulated on the dinghy bottom during our stay in Stuart. Cleaning the bottom of the dinghy on the deck of *Vagus* was not a pleasant task. Just as we finished getting the dinghy stored, a couple stopped by our boat.

"We saw you storing your dinghy. Are you going to the Bahamas?"

"Yes," replied Karen. "We plan to leave in the afternoon and head directly to Lucaya."

"So are we!" exclaimed Louie with a smile. Louie and Michelle on *Allegro* were buddy-boating with Pierre and Marsha on *Sundown*. The two couples were from Quebec and their plans for the crossing matched with ours. They even agreed with the interpretation of the weather forecast and the departure times.

"Let's keep in touch by radio and meet at the harbour entrance in Palm Beach at 5:00pm."

After they left, we looked at each other and smiled. A wave of relief washed over us. At least someone else agreed with our plans. We were either all right or all wrong, but we were not alone. It would also be nice to have someone to talk to as we made our way across. We were still quite nervous about crossing the Stream, especially after *Daydream's* experience.

Quietly we went about our individual tasks in preparing the boat for the trip. We finished early and tried to have a little rest during the afternoon. It was an enforced idleness. We had to conserve energy but were too wound up to sleep. I kept looking at the clock. It was like waiting for a bus to arrive. We wanted to get going but knew there was no point leaving earlier. Finally 4:00pm rolled around. We saw *Allegro* and *Sundown* lifting their anchors. I turned on the motor to warm the engine.

"Time to go," I called to Karen. We raised anchor and slowly made our way down the channel towards the harbour entrance. Large freighters were lined up on docks by the shore. Marinas full of boats were scattered around the harbour. It looked like a busy place. As *Allegro* and *Sundown* pulled over to another anchorage area to do a last weather check, we headed for the harbour entrance. There was a breakwater extending a good hundred meters out and rollers were coming down the channel. The water looked a little rougher than predicted, but it was always rougher close to shore. I pointed *Vagus'* bow out the channel and towards the Bahamas. We were off. We were excited and nervous. The adrenaline had kicked in. We were going to do this! When we got past the breakwater, Karen took the wheel and I went forward to raise the mainsail. The wind, as forecast, was light and on the nose, so it would be a motor sail. The mainsail up would give us a bit of extra speed and, more importantly, help stabilize *Vagus'* motion in the swells. As I raised the sail, I noticed *Vagus* had turned south. It looked like we were pointing at Miami. I could see the glow of big city lights in the distance.

I called back to Karen, "Where are you going? There is Miami ahead!"

"We are on the proper heading - 090. I'm not sure what is happening!" said Karen.

To achieve our planned course of 090 degrees, Karen had to steer 140 degrees. We did not know it at the time, but we were already in the Gulf Stream. According to the forecast, the Stream was supposed to be six miles offshore. It was, in fact, at the harbour entrance. We were now crabbing towards the Bahamas. Fortunately, the Gulf Stream was only 20 miles wide at this location. After about 5 hours, *Vagus* reached the edge of the Stream and her heading started to match the course. We started to make better speed in the desired direction. Although we were through the worst, we did not really believe it. With all the hype, we kept waiting for it to get bad. Instead, we experienced a fairly pleasant motor sail on a moonlit, starry night. We spotted a few ships but the traffic was not heavy. We could see the navigation lights of *Allegro* and *Sundown* behind us. Both boats had left about half an hour after *Vagus*. While on watch, I would look for *Allegro* and *Sundown's* navigation lights and try to keep them behind us. I found out later that they, in turn, were watching *Vagus'* lights and following us.

We tried to fall into the routine of an overnight trip and took turns trying to get some rest. It was difficult. We both were "pumped up" by the Gulf Stream crossing and excited about traveling to a new land, the Bahamas. By dawn, we were in the New Providence Channel, passing the lights of Freeport. By 8:00am, we were nearing Lucaya. We first missed the entrance. On the charts, the entrance was supposed to be marked by several large ship moorings - only the moorings were no longer there. We doubled back and spotted a small boat coming out of the land. Karen, with the binoculars, spotted a marker pole by the small boat. The entrance was right where the GPS said it was. I, however, had not trusted using only the instruments. I wanted to see where I was going. The waters of the New Providence Channel were beginning to get quite rough. With a feeling of great relief, we motored through the rock-lined entrance to the Lucayan waterway. We called in for a slip at a marina around one bend in the waterway and Karen scurried around the deck, putting out lines and fenders. As we arrived at the slip, several boaters came over to help with the lines and welcome us in. Everyone was curious.

"Where did you leave from? How was the Stream? What time did you leave?" - normal boater questions.

After tying up, I got together all the boat papers and passports to go check in. The quarantine flag flew over *Vagus* to indicate that we were not yet checked in. Only the skipper could leave the boat until the check in was completed. I walked to the marina office. It was sunny and warm. I gawked at the water in the canal. It was swimming pool clear and loaded with small fish. It was everything that it was reported to be. The office gave me some forms to fill out and told me to go back to the boat. The Customs and Immigration people were on their way and they would contact me when they arrived. Several other boats, including

*Allegro* and *Sundown*, were also waiting to check in. I walked back slowly, holding my papers and staring at the water. We were now on Bahamas time. The Customs and Immigration people showed up at noon. It was just as well. It had taken me all morning to fill out the four page detailed questionnaire. I had no idea how to answer some of the questions. I just responded and decided, if queried, to plead ignorance. The check-in, when it happened, went quickly. The officers were friendly and my answers passed. So, with a large stamp, a flourish of a signature and, of course, $300US, we were now legally in the Bahamas. We had officially arrived. I proudly showed Karen the stamped forms as soon as I returned to *Vagus*. We hugged. We were in the Bahamas! And it was New Year's Eve.

We were invited to a potluck New Year's Eve party that night at the marina. Karen prepared a dish but we would not make it. About 5:00pm, it all caught up with us. We had been up for almost thirty-six hours and the adrenaline had run out. We lay down for a nap before the party. The next morning, we woke up, refreshed, to a clear, sunny, warm New Year's Day in the Bahamas. It was a morning we would always remember.

*New Year's Day in the Bahamas!*

# Epilogue

*A* new year, a new country and new adventures – we were ready. The Bahamas were ahead of us – home of warm weather, clear water, and friendly people. We had just completed a 2000 mile trip along the eastern seaboard, picking up new skills along the way. The trip was a great teacher. It was a beautiful trip, but a tough, tiring trip - having to stay on the move to keep ahead of the cold. It would have been nice to take more time, but it was not to be. Karen learned that the difference between and ordeal and an adventure was attitude – or was it just the number of letters in the words. She was still working on that one.

The Bahamas was a major objective for us. Sitting back in the marina in Lake Ontario, it had seemed doable. However, we had questions. Could we stand living together in close quarters for 24 hours a day, or the constant struggle of looking after life's necessities while on the move, or the demands of continually facing new experiences, or being "on watch" literally 24 hours a day when on a boat? The cruising life is not for everyone. Many find the trip arduous and not up to the romantic ideals of the cruising magazine's ravings. We knew it would be a demanding trip, but we did not know if it would be a trip we would enjoy. We had discussed various contingency plans if we found the trip was not for us. And these plans were debated throughout the trip. Now we were in the Bahamas.

Once again, I had reached a new destination and realized that I had been focused on "the getting there". Now it was time to figure out what "to do there". On that beautiful, New Years morning, we knew not what lay ahead, but we were ready, or as ready as we could be. In the next book, we will explore the Bahamas, make new friends, have an offshore adventure, reunite with old friends and get into "island time" in the Windwards. A challenging time was ahead of us. The cruising life is not an easy life, but it is a rewarding life.

# Appendix A

# Vagus V - Distances Traveled

| Date | Location | Distance (nm) |
|------|----------|---------------|
| **August** | | |
| 7/8 | Cobourg, Ontario to Oswego, NY | 81.7 |
| 9 | Lock 8, Oswego, NY | 0.5 |
| 11 | Phoenix, NY | 21.0 |
| 12 | Brewerton, NY | 12.0 |
| 13 | Sylvan Beach, NY | 19.5 |
| 14 | Little Falls, NY | 43.0 |
| 16 | Fonda, NY | 25.6 |
| 17 | Lock 8, Erie Canal, NY | 19.1 |
| 18 | Waterford, NY | 30.0 |
| 20 | Catsgill Creek, NY | 35.1 |
| 23 | Poughkeepsie, NY | 28.4 |
| 24 | Nyak, NY | 49.0 |
| 25 | New York, NY | 19.8 |
| 27 | Atlantic Highlands, NJ | 24.9 |
| **September** | | |
| 7/8 | Breakwater Harbor, NJ | 135.0 |
| 11 | Chesapeake City, MD | 80.0 |
| 14 | Georgetown, MD | 32.4 |

| 15 | Baltimore, MD | 45.2 |
| 18 | "Isabel" - Baltimore | -- |
| 26 | Ridout Creek, MD | 27.1 |
| 29 | Annapolis, MD | 10.0 |

## October

| 13 | Solomons, MD | 55.0 |
| 16 | Sandy Point, VA | 48.1 |
| 17 | Deltaville, VA | 27.0 |
| 19 | Hampton, VA | 47.0 |
| 20 | Norfolk, VA | 12.4 |
| 23 | Great Bridge, VA | 11.7 |
| 24 | Buck Island, NC | 42.4 |
| 25 | Tuckahoe Point, Alligator River, NC | 46.8 |
| 26 | Dowry Creek, NC | 25.5 |
| 28 | Cedar Creek, NC | 50.7 |
| 29 | Beaufort, NC | 17.2 |
| 31 | Mile Hammond, NC | 43.0 |

## November

| 1 | Wrightsville Beach, NC | 43.0 |
| 2 | St. James, NC | 29.7 |
| 3 | Osprey Marina, SC | 54.9 |
| 4 | Georgetown, SC | 28.2 |
| 6 | Dewee Creek, SC | 49.0 |
| 7 | Charleston, SC | 16.1 |
| 10 | South Edisto River, SC | 32.4 |
| 11 | Skull Creek, Hilton Head, SC | 43.6 |
| 12 | Buckhead Creek, GA | 52.3 |
| 13 | Duplin River, GA | 39.9 |
| 14 | Delaroche Creek, GA | 50.3 |
| 15 | Jacksonville Beach, FL | 43.4 |
| 16 | St. Augustine, FL | 29.4 |
| 18 | Daytona Beach, FL | 56.6 |
| 22 | Titusville, FL | 41.9 |
| 23 | Indian Harbor, FL | 33.3 |
| 24 | Fort Pierce, FL | 47.5 |
| 25 | Stuart, FL | 27.3 |

**December**

| | | |
|---|---|---|
| 29 | Lake Worth, FL | 34.0 |
| 30/31 | Lucaya Marina Village, | |
| | Grand Bahama Island, Bahamas | 85.0 |
| | **Grand Total** | **2003.9** |

# Appendix B

# Vagus V – Equipment List

## Vagus V

- 1980 CS 36 Traditional
- length over all – 11.13m
- length water line – 8.92m
- beam – 3.50m
- draft – 1.52m
- displacement – 7021kg
- masthead to waterline – 16.11m

## Sails

- mainsail with three reefs
- No. 3 120% Genoa
- No. 3 100% Genoa hank-on
- storm Jib (hank-on)
- Asymmetrical cruising spinnaker

## Rigging

- anodized aluminum keel-steeped 16.58m mast
- anodized aluminum boom with four internal reefing lines and topping lift
- 1 x 19 stainless steel shrouds and stays: uppers, intermediates and fore and aft lowers
- insulated backstay

# Deck

- 2 genoa halyards and 2 spinnaker halyards
- boom vang
- Lifesling
- Avon 4-man Offshore life raft
- Aerogen 6 wind generator
- 2 x Shell Solar 55 watt solar panels
- dinghy motor hoist on wind generator support
- canvas dodger and bimini – full plastic or mosquito net zip-on enclosures
- Magma propane barbeque

# Anchors and Equipment

- 22 kg Bruce anchor with 65m high tensile 5/16" chain
- 9kg aluminum Spade anchor with 15m 3/8" chain and 45m 5/8" rope
- Fortress FX-23 anchor with 15m 5/16" high tensile chain and 60m 5/8" rope
- Fortress FX-7 kedge anchor with 3m 5/16in chain and 45m 1/2" rope
- 3lb Danforth dinghy anchor with 2m 5/16in chain and 30m 1/2" rope
- anchor windlass – Muir H-1200
- Galerider drogue
- 9ft parachute anchor with swivel and 90m 5/8" double braid rope
- 3.1m Avon Rover inflatable dinghy
- 8Hp Yamaha 2 stroke outboard motor

# Self-steering

- Sailomat 601 self steering windvane
- Autohelm 3000
- Navico TP10 (for Sailomat)

## Engine, Batteries and Systems

- Westerbeke 30 diesel engine– 30Hp
- aluminum fuel tank – 159 l.
- house batteries - 4 x T105 Trojan 6V golf cart batteries
- starter battery – Trojan Group 27
- 90 amp alternator with three stage regulator
- fresh water tanks – 372 l.
- hot water tank – 22 l.
- waste tank – 145 l.

## Electrics and Electronics

- Cetrec knot log and depth sounder
- SR wind speed and direction
- Raytheon chart plotter, radar dome and WAAS GPS
- Ham radio system – Icom 706 MKIIG transceiver , SCS Pactor Modem and Icom tuner
- VHF radio – Icom M402 with cockpit remote
- handheld VHF radio – Garmin 725
- ACR 406 EPIRB
- Pur 40  watermaker
- Adler Barber cold plate 12V refrigerator

# Appendix C

# List of Charts and Guides

## Charts and Guide Books used from Lake Ontario to the Bahamas

### Charts

- Richardson's Chart Book – Hudson River and Adjacent Waterways
- WC 56 Cape May – Sandy Hook
- 12327 New York Harbour
- Maptech Chartkit, Chesapeake and Delaware Bays
- The ICW Chartbook
- Maptech Chartkit, Norfolk, VA to Florida and the ICW
- Maptech Chartkit, Jacksonville to Miami
- Explorer Chartbook, Near Bahamas
- Explorer Chartbook, Far Bahamas
- Explorer Chartbook, Exumas

# Guides

- Skipper Bob's New York Canal System
- Shellenberger - Cruising the Chesapeake, a Gunkholer's Guide
- Chesapeake Bay Magazine's Guide to Cruising Chesapeake Bay
- Waterway Guide, Mid-Atlantic, Chesapeake Bay and the ICW to Florida
- Skipper Bob's Anchorages along the ICW
- Skipper Bob's Marinas Along the ICW
- Intracoastal Waterway Norfolk to Miami
- Embassy Guide - Florida's East Coast
- Waterway Guide Southern 2004, Florida, the Gulf of Mexico, and the Bahamas
- Skipper Bob's Bahamas Bound
- Cruising Guide to Abaco Bahamas 2004 - Dodge
- On and Off the Beaten Path  - Pavlidis
- The Exuma Guide – Pavlidis

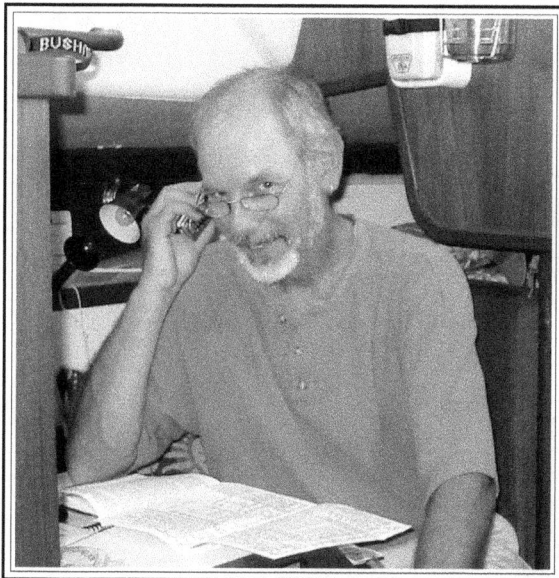

## <u>About the Author</u>

Jim started life as a child – at least his first memories are of himself as a child – and a happy one at that. With his family grown and his job behind him, life aboard his sailing yacht *Vagus V* continued to allow that happy child to play. A four year sailing adventure with his wife, Karen, took him from Lake Ontario, through the Caribbean, and back. Now, at his home in Burlington, Ontario, he tries to collect some random thoughts on his laptop computer and push them out on the unsuspecting world.